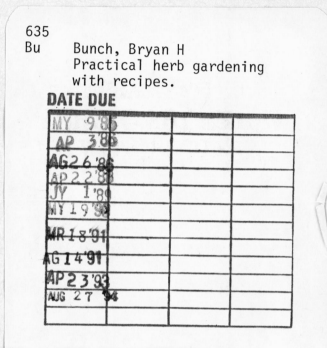

PRACTICAL
HERB GARDENING
WITH RECIPES

BY BRYAN H. BUNCH
A HUDSON GROUP BOOK
ILLUSTRATIONS BY LESLIE TIERNEY

TAB BOOKS Inc.
BLUE RIDGE SUMMIT, PA. 17214

FIRST EDITION

FIRST PRINTING

Copyright © 1984 by TAB BOOKS Inc.

Printed in the United States of America

Library of Congress Cataloging in Publication Data

Bunch, Bryan H.
    Practical herb gardening—with recipes.

    "A Hudson Group book."
    Includes index.
    1. Herb gardening. 2. Cookery (Herbs) 3. Organic
gardening. I. Title.
SB351.H5B86 1984   635'.7   83-24233
ISBN 0-8306-0661-0
ISBN 0-8306-1661-6 (pbk.)
Cover illustration by Al Cozzi.

Contents

Introduction

There are seemingly a million books about herbs, as well there should be because herbs are endlessly fascinating. Yet, with all those books, there seems to be not one that tells you how to grow herbs and how to use them in cooking—their greatest glory. This book is devoted to filling that need.

Most herb books bog down in details of herb history and lore, most of it unproven. Each author seems to have taken two or three dozen different books that have different points of view, and picked up, more or less at random, the bits of herb myth that appealed to him. How else could you account for the same book telling you that a given herb is a laxative, a digestive, an aphrodisiac, suitable for borders, and frequently used with fish?

You cannot avoid herb lore, and I have included some of the best-documented or most-interesting stories—but they are really beside the point. Herbs are easy to grow, and fresh herbs are necessary for elegant cooking. That is the point. Many herbs once common to most gardens have limited use in today's cooking. This book focuses on those herbs that have the widest use in recipes and that can be grown easily with small investments of space, time, and money by amateur gardeners.

The basis of my advice about growing herbs is my own experience, although over the years I have learned a great deal from books, magazines, and other gardeners. These ideas are included because they work. Because I am a longtime believer in *organic gardening,* there is a distinct organic basic noticeable—but my experience, as well as that of millions of other gardeners, is that organic gardening is the most practical course for the backyard gardener.

Perennial herbs are more practical in a small garden than annual or biennial herbs, and you will find directions for planning a perennial herb garden and for growing these long-lived herbs. The popular annuals and biennials are also covered, as well as herbs used for tea. Harvesting and drying methods are described, and there is a chapter detailing indoor herbs.

All of the recipes are my adaptations of fairly standard dishes, with the focus on the ones that I like to eat frequently. Consequently, there is an emphasis on healthy food, with an occasional treat that one cannot resist.

No one can write a useful nonfiction book without help. I particularly want to thank my wife, Mary, for reading the manuscript and making many useful comments—and for weeding my gardens. I also want to thank Leslie Tierney for providing the illustrations, and for her constant checking of the growing herbs in the garden to make sure that she had captured the essence of each type.

For my father
in whose gardens I grew up.

Chapter 1
Herbs

It is not clear what a herb is or how to say the word. Nevertheless, it *is* clear that herbs are regaining the popularity they once had. Books about herbs flood bookstores. Magazines tell you in a few pithy words and a lot of beautiful pictures that you should grow a few herbs around the house. There are herbal shampoos and lotions of all kinds.

A typical response to all this occurred the other day when I mentioned to a new acquaintance that I was writing a book about herb gardening and cooking with herbs. He said, "I like herbs. I don't know much about them, but I like them."

What's not to like?

Herbs are small, attractive plants that have been used by human beings as long as there have been human beings. They make soothing teas, they give flavor and fragrance to all sorts of food, and they can even be good for you. Herbs are easy to grow and present few of the problems that vegetables or flowers do.

WHAT IS A HERB?

Herbs are not well defined. To a botanist, a herb is a flowering plant that dies back to the ground in the winter. Some would further divide this classification into the *forbs* and the grasses, calling only the forbs—that is, any botanical herb that is not a grass—herbs. Although this definition is quite specific, it includes far too many plants that most people would not call herbs and excludes various plants that most people would call herbs.

Another approach is to say that a herb is any plant for which a part of the plant is valued for its flavor, fragrance, dye, or medicinal use. Although this approach includes all the plants that most people think of as herbs, it also includes a lot of other plants that most would reject. Is a truffle a herb? Is a nutmeg tree a herb? What about a honeysuckle vine? Or a tomato? A willow? Yet truffles, tomatoes, and nutmeg are all used for flavoring. Honeysuckle has a terrific fragrance; tomato paste is sometimes used for coloring foods; and willow bark can be chewed or brewed as a headache cure.

No satisfactory definition will ever be given for *herb* because the word refers to a general idea that can change from time to time. For this book, however, I define *herb* as a small plant that can be grown in a temperate climate and whose leaves, seeds, or bulbs are used primarily for flavoring food or making tea. I am not dealing with plants that are used primarily for medicinal or dyeing purposes. However, for completeness, some of these other plants can be mentioned in the course of a discussion.

The restriction to a temperate climate is important for several reasons. Tropical-plant seeds or fruit used for flavoring food are generally called *spices*. The infusion of tropical true tea or coffee is not the same thing as a herb tea, although only by custom. Because this is a practical book, and because it is aimed at people in the United States, there would be no point in discussing extensively how to grow tropical plants.

By small plants, I mean plants that are shorter than I am, or under 6 feet tall. Otherwise, it would be difficult to exclude certain trees, such as the sassafras. The only true tree to be considered is the bay tree, but when it is grown in a tub in the northern United States, it stays within the 6-foot height limitation.

Of course, many vegetables that are not herbs are involved in flavoring food. The distinction between an onion and garlic, or between celery and lovage, or between broccoli and capers, or between peas and caraway is as much a matter of tradition as anything else. The foundation of the distinction would appear to be that you eat vegetables by themselves, while herbs are almost always used as flavoring.

A PRONUNCIATION NOTE

Some people pronounce the *h* in *herb* and some people do not. I pronounce the *h* some of the time and drop it some of the time, depending on my mood. In the manuscript for this book I have tried to follow the usage common to most people who grow herbs, which is to write "a herb" instead of "an herb."

As the story goes, the word was originally pronounced "erb," but class-conscious people in England started saying "herb" so they would not sound cockney. I have some trouble accepting this theory. My understanding of cockney is that an *h* sound is added to words that start with a vowel, so a cockney speaker, hearing "erb", would say "herb." Nevertheless, that is the story.

In the United States, most educated people, not worried about sounding cockney, still say "erb," while partly educated people, seeing the *h*, say "herb." Why gardeners who grow herbs lean toward "herb" instead of "erb" is anybody's guess.

My dictionary, like me, straddles the fence, giving "(h)erb" as the pronunciation guide.

SORT OF A HISTORY

Anthropological research does not reveal the origin of herbs in cooking, so one can only imagine the scene of discovery. Granted, this origin is not quite so significant as the discovery of how to light a fire or the invention of the wheeled vehicle, but it is worth contemplating in any case.

It seems highly probable that the medicinal uses of herbs preceded their use as flavoring. Most of the early writers on herbs emphasize the value of herbs in healing, although some herbs were already recognized as flavors quite early as well. It also seems likely that plants originally eaten for their flavor were the precursors of vegetables, not herbs.

In the beginning, before food was cooked at all, it is unlikely that two foods or two flavors were ever combined. When cooking first started, people would not have known how to change the flavor. Early cooking probably consisted largely of roasting or broiling, techniques that would encourage cooking single meats, fish, or vegetables without adding other flavors.

When boiling (or simmering or braising) was invented, cooking may have taken a different turn. Nothing could be more natural than to add to the same pot several items that were being cooked, thus saving on pots and getting the best use of the fire. The invention of stew may have come as a surprise. Each food flavored the others, and they all flavored the sauce.

Still, it is a long way from cooking foods together that you are used to eating separately to adding to a food a small amount of a plant that you would be unlikely to eat by itself. Putting all these ideas together, you can imagine a scene such as the following:

Mulki not only led the women in their searches for roots, seeds, berries, and slow games (such as turtles, snakes, frogs, and hedgehogs) and whole band when they moved from camp to camp, but she was also the keeper of the secret information about plants. The secret information consisted of the knowledge of which plants could produce visions, cure illnesses, induce abortions, and produce sleep. Some plants were much more powerful than others. In some, the leaves were powerful but the roots worthless; in others the power was in the roots or the seeds, while the leaves shared only a little of the power.

When her husband complained of indigestion, Mulki made him chew seeds that she had gathered the year before from a feathery plant that grew in patches in the meadows. Her husband did not like the taste very much—too strong—so he only pretended to chew them, and he spit them out as soon as he could. Mulki saw through his pretense very easily, especially since her husband did not seem to be eating with his usual abandon. She was determined to help him in spite of himself.

She began to add small amounts of the much less powerful leaves from the same feathery plant to foods of all kinds. At first, the medicinal plant could not be tasted at all. Gradually she increased the amount of leaves to the point at which she was just able to recognize the flavor of the feathery plant in the food. Mulki knew it was helping, for her husband and her whole family soon were enjoying food more than ever. By the time she had increased the amount of leaves enough that anyone could taste them, there were no complaints; on the contrary, Mukli and her whole family preferred the food with the medicine in it to the food without it they had been used to.

Mukli begain to experiment with other plants that were not so powerful that they could harm her family. Many of these improved the taste of the food, although many did not. When Mulki passed on the secret information to her daughter, she also passed on the secret of using herbs in cooking.

That's only a fantasy, of course, but some part of it is probably true. There are other ways in which early people could have discovered the benefits of herbs. Some woody herbs, for example, such as thyme or rosemary, impart some of their flavor when foods are roasted or broiled over fires that include the herbs as fuel. A logical step would be to check out the leaves or other parts of the plants for

4

flavoring. Animals that feed heavily on a particular herb may pick up a little of the herb's flavor in their flesh, another possible connection to be made.

Certainly the use of herbs as medicine was known from the time of the earliest written records we have. A common theme for herb gardens is to plant all the herbs listed in the Bible, one of the earliest documents. A Chinese list of herbs dated at around 2700 B.C. lists a herb for every day of the year, although it focuses on medicinal uses only.

Because of their medicinal properties, herbs are thought by some to be the earliest cultivated plants, although this seems unlikely to me. From early times, the flavoring qualities of herbs were well known. Most herbs were valued for both the flavor and the curative or magical properties they were supposed to have.

Yet, times have brought herbs into and out of prominence over and over again. Although the Greeks and Romans knew the flavoring potential of herbs, the Mediterranean herbs were often pushed aside by the arrival of imported spices. In medieval times, when the spices were no longer available, the use of native herbs experienced a resurgence, while the more exotic herbs were kept only in monastery gardens. The invention of printing brought the golden age of herbs, for it seemed that everyone who could do so wrote a herbal.

When the first Colonists came to America, they brought herbs with them, but as people in the United States lost faith in the medicinal properties of herbs, they also lost touch with herbs as flavorings. Not so the makers of processed food, who continued to use herbs in all sorts of food to make it more palatable. In Europe, herbs grown at home or sold in markets were more common, however, so when American soldiers were exposed to European cooking during two world wars, they brought back a taste for better-flavored food.

The latest herb breakthrough, however, came from the environmental movement. As people rebelled against the damage that was being done to the environment, they also turned away from overprocessed foods and looked for natural alternatives—which leads us back to the current revival of interest in herbs.

WHAT IS A "PRACTICAL" HERB?

This book details, for inexperienced gardeners or cooks, gardening and cooking techniques using herbs. No matter which definition of herb is used, there are many more herbs available than can be grown in any but the largest gardens. Besides, many herbs are little used in cooking any more or never were. Therefore, the focus of this book is on those herbs that can conveniently be grown in a small garden by the average person and that will have some impact on a wide range of recipes. These herbs are discussed in detail several places in the book, depending on the topic.

There is no effort made to be encyclopedic, although I frequently give lists of herbs having a particular trait, lists that go well beyond the basic 25 herbs that receive detailed treatment. If you want to find out whether a particular herb is an annual or a perennial, whether it can be grown indoors, whether or not it is used in teas, whether it has medicinal value, or something else, the chances are good that you will find the herb in the index, where you will be referred to the appropriate list in the body of the book. In this way, I can give detailed accounts (in a small book) for the herbs a person is likely to grown or use and at the same time I can provide the key information for dozens of other herbs.

The main herbs given more extended treatment are those that are generally grown and used in the United States: basil, bay, caraway, chives, coriander, dill, garlic, marjoram, mint, oregano, parsley, rosemary, sage, tarragon, and thyme. Almost as much space is devoted to another group of herbs that are representative of more of the range of herbs available: chamomile, chervil, comfrey, cumin, Egyptian onions, fennel, lemon balm, lovage, nasturtium, and winter savory.

The most practical herbs for someone with a small garden are the perennials, and the longest single section of the book details how to plan a perennial herb garden, prepare the soil, and grow the herbs. Annuals, biennials, and other herbs treated as annuals get a chapter of their own. The chapter on herb teas includes a good deal more than just the teas, since it deals with harvesting and storing herbs. People who discover how much better fresh herbs are than dried herbs, however, will want to bring their herbs into the house for the winter; this is the main focus of the chapter on indoor herbs.

Nothing beats the experience of actually growing your own herbs in helping you to sort out the ways of dealing with a particular situation. Since I cannot give someone that experience, I do the next best thing by telling of some of my own experiences. These are grouped in the Encounters with Herbs chapter along with notes about the herbs gleaned from reading about them, from talking to other gardeners, and from visiting other herb gardens. Nearly all of the Encounters end with a brief, informal recipe that brings out the character of the herb.

Finally, since a herb is not practical unless there is some use to which it can be put, a collection of recipes in which herbs play an important part is given. These recipes are grouped in the traditional way, as a several-course meal, rather than by the predominate herb used. One reason is that in most cases, the herbs are not supposed to be predominate. A recipe nearly always features several herbs used in conjunction. The other reason for grouping in this way is that most people consult recipe lists in order to find something to cook, not to find some way to use a herb that they happen to have on hand.

Chapter 2
The No-Work, Perennial Herb Garden

The first and easiest kind of herb garden for anyone interested primarily in herbs for cooking is a perennial garden. *Perennials* are simply those plants that live more than two years—or that seem to live more than two years—because of their growth habits. In some cases, the actual parent plant may not survive but is succeeded instead by daughter plants in the same spot every year, so the effect is the same as a single plant that has a long life. A clump of plants that replaces itself in this way may live indefinitely, while a single plant will eventually succumb to some disaster or another.

For various reasons, mostly misguided, perennials have been somewhat out of favor with American gardeners in the twentieth century; they have been the mainstay of English gardens and were previously the foundation of American flower and herb gardens. This century-long trend now seems to be ending, partly as a result of the environmental movement and perhaps partly as a result of the economy. Annual plants, those that must be planted from seed every year, are throwaway plants, like nonreturnable bottles. Perennials recycle themselves. Even in vegetable gardens, long the almost exclusive domain of the annuals, perennials are making a comeback. There are even breeders working now on developing perennial varieties of field crops such as corn and wheat.

The economy certainly favors the renewed interest in perennials. Inflation has dramatically raised the price of seeds. The oil crisis has raised the price of oil-based fertilizers even more. Once a perennial has been started, it costs little to maintain year after year. Furthermore, nearly all perennials can be propagated vegetatively, that is, new plants can be grown from parts of existing plants. Even if you buy a single plant to start with, you can, within a year or two, produce enough young plants from the first to fill out an extensive garden.

In fact, the problem with nearly all of the perennial herbs (after you get the first plant) is to prevent new plants from springing up or to find sensible ways to dispose of the parts of existing plants that can be planted to form new plants. In fact, if you know someone who already grows a perennial herb, you can nearly always obtain your starting plants free.

The techniques that work well for the small-scale herb gardener do not always translate into techniques that are useful for large-scale growers. Perhaps this is one of the reasons that it is almost impossible to find fresh perennial herbs for use in cooking in the produce departments of grocery stores or markets. Some annual or biennial herbs that are often used in quantity, such as parsley, dill, basil, or coriander, may appear in markets, but it is extremely difficult or impossible to find the perennials, such as thyme, tarragon, oregano, or sage, in any form but dried.

Another factor, however, is that most of the perennial herbs are used in very small quantities. It would be difficult to justify the purchase of a bunch of thyme when all you really need is just a sprig. Therefore, if you want to use fresh perennial herbs in your cooking, it is necessary to grow them in your garden or to hope that your neighbor will grow them.

You certainly do want to use the fresh herbs if you care about cooking and fresh taste. Although dried herbs have their uses, these uses are not the same as for fresh herbs. For example, a single dried bay leaf has little flavor, but if you use more dried bay leaves in an attempt to improve the flavor, you end up with an unpleasant mess, suddenly tasting far too strongly of bay. A fresh bay leaf, on the other hand, contributes just the right touch of the flavor of bay with none of the unpleasant overtones. Similarly, while you might put a pinch or two of dried herbs in a salad dressing, the effects is nowhere near the same as mixing a few fresh leaves in the salad itself. Dried rosemary leaves are like short little spears that do not get any softer or less sharp in cooking. Fresh rosemary, especially if it is new growth, is a soft leaf that merges imperceptibly, except for the flavor, into the texture of the dish. For serious cooking and serious enjoyment of the result you *need* fresh herbs.

Fortunately, having fresh herbs available is the easiest goal in gardening to attain. If you spend a little time preparing the soil properly, most of your perennial herbs will require almost no care thereafter—no weeding, no spraying, no watering, no fertilizing; no care at all except (in many climates) covering the herbs in the fall with a protective mulch and removing the mulch in the spring.

Also, the space requirement for a perennial herb garden is incredibly small. It is possible to grow the eight most essential cooking herbs in a space that is smaller than a cemetery plot. Should you not have that much available space in one place, you can grow each herb in its own spot scattered about a yard, one plant taking at the most a square foot. In either case, you will also be contributing to the aesthetic quality of your life, for the perennial herbs are attractive plants. Many are grown in gardens for their looks alone.

Most of the preceding assumes that you want to spend as little money, time, and space as possible on your herb garden. In fact, that is the basic theme of this book, but I hope that you will find that growing herbs is so rewarding that you will want to go into it more deeply. Herbs can be and are grown in elaborate arrangements, such as knot gardens, that become major landscaping elements. There are hundreds of species and varieties of herbs and related plants that a person can grow if he or she decides to make a major hobby out of the experience. The advice given here will apply to those situations, also, but the central aim is to develop a *practical* herb garden, not a hobbyist's or specialist's garden.

SITING THE GARDEN

With all that in mind, the remainder of this chapter is devoted to the proper procedures for starting and maintaining 14 perennial herbs. Further thoughts on growing and using each of the herbs are found in the chapter "Encounters with Herbs." Most of the problems and procedures for growing perennial herbs are common to all 14, however, so it makes more sense to group the general advice here.

For the record, the 14 perennial herbs that are included in this guide are:

bay	mint
chamomile	oregano
chives	rosemary
comfrey	sage
Egyptian onions	tarragon

lemon balm	thyme
lovage	winter savory

Although this list is not exhaustive, it is too long for most people. Horseradish, woodruff, Good King Henry, costmary, chicory, saffron, cardoon, hyssop, elecampane, lemon verbena, garlic, horehound, bee balm, sweet cicely, catnip, sorrel, salad burnet, and even dandelion, which are also perennial herbs with some values in cooking or making herbal teas, are therefore omitted. Depending on the amount of use you make of herbs, you can usually get by with half or less of the list of 14. In northern climates (north of Washington, DC, roughly), bay and rosemary need special care; therefore you might want to strike them from the list.

Chamomile, comfrey, lemon balm, and mint are mainly used in teas; if that is not a principal interest of yours, they can go. Egyptian onions, lovage, and winter savory have somewhat specialized uses. Furthermore, Egyptian onions and lovage consume rather more space than the other herbs. You might not want to deal with them. This leaves as an almost irreducible minimum:

chives
oregano
sage
tarragon
thyme

If you go for the minimum, then, you can have a perennial herb garden that is about 6 feet long and 2 feet wide. If possible, however, you should allow a little more room and grow one, two, or more of the others.

Look around your yard for a suitable site. The two principal requirements are sunlight and good drainage; soil can always be improved. You should avoid sites as much as possible that may be invaded by the roots of trees or shrubs. Most cooks find it best if the garden has easy access from the kitchen, although it is more important to deal with sunlight, drainage, and roots before dealing with access. A garden outside the kitchen door that fails to flourish is not much use.

Sun

Herbs require at least six hours of sunlight each day during the growing season, but do better if they get more. Sunlight, after all, is the basic food of green plants. The chemicals that they take from the soil are like the vitamins and minerals in our food—essential but not nourishing. Expecting a plant to grow and flourish without sunlight is like expecting a child to grow on a diet of daily pills with no other food. It won't work.

You can check the amount of sunlight that is available in your yard simply by watching the shadows, but remember that the sun moves around in the sky from season to season and that the amount of shade produced by trees and bushes changes also. The amount of shade in the winter has nothing to do with the amount that will exist when your trees are in the full leaf of summer. Since a perennial garden is intended to occupy the same site for years (even generations), you need to plan for sunlight years ahead also. A small oak tree 20 feet away may not shade the herbs this year, but what is it going to be like 10 or 20 years down the line?

Planning for sunlight is not always easy. Unless you have lived in the same place for a few years and noticed how the sun affected the various parts of your yard, you may have to resort to mathematics—the last resort of a gardener—to determine which parts of the yard will get enough sunlight.

On your side will be the fact that the sun is higher in the sky in the summer—when it is most needed. At that time of the year, it has generally moved toward a path that tends toward rising in the northeast and setting in the northwest, while in the winter the sun tends to rise in the southeast and set in the southwest. Charts exist that will give the exact position of the sun in the sky all year at various longitudes if you need more detailed information (a good source is a book about designing passive solar houses).

In any case, if you are doing the planning for your garden in January (as many gardeners do), the pattern of sunlight in your yard can be inferred, but not observed. Assume that large objects, such as your house or your neighbor's, will cast shorter shadows in the summer; watch out for deciduous trees that will leaf out later in the year; and expect the sun to be farther north in the summer than it is in the winter. If you cannot get a full day of sunlight, at least try for six to eight hours a day.

If you have no such spot available, do not lose heart. The Chelsea Physic Garden in London reports that they have had success growing such Mediterranean herbs as thyme, sage, rosemary, and summer savory in light shade as long as the soil drained very well. In some ways, this combination reflects the growing conditions found in the natural habitats of these herbs. Most of these herbs are in the mint family, and the true mints are even better adapted to shade. In fact, the best place to grow peppermint, spearmint, and the like is in a partially shaded spot where the soil is always moist. The American mint known as bee balm (to herb growers; flower gardeners are apt to call it monarda after its genus) is also happy in the shade. I did not know this and kept it in full sun for several years. Then a change in the gardening plan seemed to require that I discard it—but I never throw anything away. So I planted it in a spot that I thought was too shady for flowering herbs, where it did as well, or perhaps better, than in the sun. Chives will also grow in partial shade, although they may not flower as well as in the sunlight.

Drainage

After sunlight, the most important part of siting a perennial herb garden is adequate drainage. Inadequate drainage can be corrected—with difficulty—but it is essential that herbs (and most other plants) not be planted in soggy soil. Sage, which is often a hard herb to keep going, is particularly likely to expire after a year or two if the drainage is poor. Only the true mints seem to enjoy soil that is always damp. It is easier to correct a sandy soil that drains too fast than it is to solve the problem of a clayey soil or a soil with a clay or rock base that holds standing water.

Many of the herbs that we are accustomed to using in cooking are originally from seaside locations. Very few are from swamps. The roots of common herbs need the oxygen from the air that a well-drained soil provides. They are not equipped to pull the oxygen from water the way that swamp-based plants are. In fact, some of the seaside plants, such as rosemary, are extremely sensitive to water. Rosemary, for example, dies quickly if it is allowed either to become too moist or too dry. Its ancestors were accustomed to the continual moisture supplied by the Mediterranean and to the easy drainage of seaside soils. Since our cooking heritage is largely from France and Italy, with some intrusions from Greece, Germany, and England, a lot of the common herbs are sensitive to water in this way. Much of each of these countries is close to the sea.

It is easier to tell if your potential herb-garden site has good drainage than it is to tell if it has adequate sunlight. If water stands on the site at any time of the year (most commonly in the late winter or early spring), the drainage is poor. Another check is to dig a hole 5 or 6 inches deep in the prospective site, and wait until a heavy rainstorm. If the hole still has standing water a day after the rain,

13

you have a problem. Lacking rain, you can fill the hole with a hose and see how it drains, although the results will not be so clear-cut, for the soil that is around the hole may accept water when it is dry but refuse it when the soil is wet from rain.

If the soil fails one or more of these tests, but is otherwise the only good sunny place for the herb garden, there are often steps you can take to improve the situation enough to plant herbs. The worst and least improvable situation is if the soil that does not drain is also the lowest place in the yard or the lowest place for some feet around the site—but even that is not impossible to deal with. A better situation occurs if the site with poor drainage is on some kind of a slope or otherwise higher ground than the region around it. Less work is needed to correct the problem on a slope than at the bottom of an incipient lake.

There are three strategies to use to deal with poor drainage. The first, and most obvious, is to avoid poor drainage in the first place. If you can find a sunny spot with good drainage, then the rest of this section can be skipped. On the other hand, if you have a situation like mine, then you are going to have to take some additional steps. Nearly all of my backyard becomes a shallow pond for about a month each year. Consequently, I have had to solve the problem using the other strategies.

The other two strategies must be used together. One of them is to improve the soil where the herbs will be planted so that it will retain enough water but not too much. The second is to provide a place for the improved soil to shed its excess water.

Soil can be improved by adding organic materials to it or—in the case of very heavy, clayey soils—by adding sand. Sand is not as good an idea as organic material for various reasons, but it sometimes is useful. Beach sand is not usually suitable because of the salt it may contain. Therefore you need to buy sand especially for the purpose of putting it in the garden, which adds to the expense. Also, sand merely contributes to improved drainage, but organic material both improves drainage and contributes to the "vitamins and minerals" content of the soil. Organic material has the amazing capability to make sandy soils hold more water and to make clay soils shed water. It can be used no matter what your soil is like.

The most useful organic material is compost. Ways of making compost are discussed later in this chapter under "Compost". Compost has the ability to hold the *right* amount of water—not too much and not too little. Other organic materials may tend to reduce drainage when wet and then dry out in a way that is also not healthy

14

for plants. Peat moss is a good example. Damp peat moss holds too much water, but dry peat moss tends to shed water too fast. Compost balances out the water in the soil. Therefore, adding a substantial amount of compost to the soil is the best method of improving drainage.

However, sand, compost, or anything else cannot do much about drainage in a small herb garden if there is no place for excess water to flow. Depending on how poor the drainage situation is, there are several different steps you can take to improve drainage in a poor site. If the site is not very poor (this is a good idea even in an ideal site), you can make a bed that has a D-shaped cross section. The edges of the bed should be an inch or two below the surrounding soil, while the middle of the bed should be an inch or two above the soil surrounding the bed. This is the common method of handling perennial beds in England, and it not only improves drainage, but also improves the look of the bed and makes it easier to trim around.

If the site is on a small slope, you can terrace it. Water will drain from the terrace onto the slope below. You can improve a terrace somewhat by digging a ditch just below the terrace and filling it with small stones. This will have the effect of draining the deeper part of the soil that would not be touched by simple terracing.

Finally, if the garden is on a low spot that does not drain well, raise it. A raised garden has many advantages, including ease of harvesting, but its principal advantage is that it drains on all four sides (at least for the several inches it is raised above the soil). In general, you are better off with a raised or terraced garden, even if one is not necessary at your site, although the initial amount of labor may not be to your taste.

Gardens can be raised with borders of stone or treated wood. Anywhere from 4 to 8 inches is suitable. One way to get the soil needed to raise a garden is to dig a ditch around the outside of the garden and put the material from the ditch into the garden. The ditch can then be filled with porous material, such as small stones, gravel, or sand. As with a ditch in front of a terrace, this provides additional drainage at deeper levels and also makes it easier to keep the garden border trimmed of weeds. If the ditch is about a foot wide and filled with stones or sand, one wheel of the lawnmower can ride on the stones or sand, effectively eliminating the need for trimming around the raised bed. I have a very rocky soil; therefore I get enough small rocks from cultivating the soil to fill the ditch. This procedure has the added benefit of reducing the amount of rocks that

I would otherwise have to hide or haul away. It does not eliminate the problem, because the larger rocks (larger than my fist, approximately) do not go into the ditch. You get more space for the excess water by using many small rocks than you do by using fewer large rocks.

PREPARING THE SOIL

It is a common myth that herbs do better in poor soil. All plants grow better in soil that contains proper nutrients and has the appropriate drainage. It is true that some plants survive poor soil better than other plants do. Herbs that have their ancestry by the seaside can thrive in soil that may be too sandy for other plants. Sometimes poor soil can have a desirable effect. For example, nasturtiums thrive too well in good soil. Viewed anthropomorphically, the nasturtium seems to think "this soil is so good, I don't need to make much seed, for any seeds will thrive in this good soil." So it does not put forth many blossoms, although it grows to a large size with many leaves.

While the nasturtium is one of the more extreme practitioners of this tendency, all green plants will put forth leaves at the expense of blossoms and fruit when the supply of nitrogen in the soil (a principal determiner of whether the soil is "good" or "poor") is too great. Since the most valued parts of most of the perennial herbs are the leaves, this tendency poses no problem for the herb gardener. A soil that is high in nitrogen will produce more leaves.

There may be some truth to the rumor that the flavor of herbs grown in a poor soil is stronger than that of herbs grown in good soil. The essential oils that provide the flavor and fragrance may build up in leaves that grow more slowly. But it is not worth it to try for this effect because the herbs will be so small and progress so poorly. It is far better to have more of the herb; simply use more of it if the flavor is somewhat diminished.

Given these considerations, preparing the soil properly is important for any type of herb garden. For a perennial herb garden, however, it is even more essential, since the soil, once prepared, will be largely undisturbed and unchanged for the life of the garden. Your annual garden can be adjusted every year. While you can add amendments to the soil—and should—in the top inch or two of the perennial garden, the roots of most herbs are far below the top few inches and they require good growing conditions deep down there in the ground.

16

Since you can only do this task once, it is really worthwhile to make a good job of it. This means work. But I promise you that a perennial herb garden built along the lines described here will continue year after year with no additional heavy labor. If your climate is sufficiently mild, you won't have any additional work at all most years. For a small, perennial herb garden, the initial labor can be accomplished in an afternoon, even if the bed has to be raised or terraced.

Digging

In most of what follows, I have assumed that you are going to prepare a raised or terraced bed. But even if the garden is going to be level with the soil around it, the first step—after laying out the garden in the size and shape you want—is the same. You should dig the area where the garden will be. If the area is later raised, then additional soil will go on top of soil that was previously dug. The turned-over soil below provides better drainage, improved soil to a greater depth, and a thicker layer of topsoil—all to the good for the garden.

While you can dig with a tiller (a mechanical device somewhat like a power mower), for a small garden or a new garden, I expect that you will use a spade or garden fork. The method described here applies to digging a garden with a spade, which I find to be both easier and more effective than using a fork. If your soil is quite rocky, you may find that a tiller is not very useful in any case.

Unless the site was used as another kind of garden recently, the soil is likely to be covered with turf or some other kind of plant cover. Most people prefer to remove this cover and get rid of it in some way (for example, toss it into a compost pile). The advantage to doing this is that it eliminates a few weed seeds and most plants that can spring forth from buried roots (such as dandelions). The process of removing the cover can be the heaviest work of preparing the garden, however, so I usually do not do it.

If you start the garden the year before you plant it, you can simply dig the turf into the garden and let it decay, which both contributes good organic material to the soil and gets rid of the turf without hauling. This method also prevents you from removing the best part of the topsoil, for the very best topsoil tends to cling to the turf.

Many people find it difficult to plan sufficiently in advance to dig the year before. But even if you are going to dig today and plant tomorrow, you can leave the turf buried in a raised bed, especially if the bed is raised more than 4 or 5 inches. That leaves most of the weed seeds and roots too far below the surface to poke through. Roots of the herbs planted several inches above will not reach the turf level right away; in any case, the roots can usually find places to break through the turned-over turf until it decays completely into compost.

You need to dig at ground level in any case. It is not a good idea simply to dump topsoil on top of undug turf in a raised or terraced bed. The reason is that most soil has been compacted by passing traffic over the years; that is, by lawn mowers, children playing, and people walking over it. Plants will grow better in soil that has been loosened by digging than in compacted soil. The deeper the soil is loosened, the more easily roots will penetrate and the better drainage you will have. So, whether you remove the turf or dig it in, you need to dig into the soil below the turf.

This task can be made much easier and more effective by using a special technique for digging, which I first learned from seeing James Crockett. He demonstrated the method on his "Victory Garden" television show. Before changing to Crockett's procedure, it took me at least twice as much time to dig a plot as it does now; the soil was not loosened as well; and I was stiff and sore for several days after. Now I enjoy the process of digging as much as any part of gardening, a taste that many of my friends think is a bit peculiar. I can't guarantee that if you use this method you will enjoy it, but I can promise less backache and better results.

The basic idea is to avoid lifting heavy clumps of soil up into the air to turn them over. Working against the force of gravity is the hardest part of the task, so you should try to minimize it. A second goal is to avoid breaking the soil loose from the undug area that surrounds it. This is especially important if you have elected to leave turf in place. In rocky soil, the third important goal is to have some open space into which rocks can be moved, for otherwise they are great impediments to digging.

You can achieve these goals by digging along the face of a ditch. Instead of lifting the soil into the air, you merely toss it to the other side of the ditch. Since the clump you are digging is attached to nothing at the face of the ditch, you have removed some of the resistance to being dug. Finally, medium-size rocks will slip into the ditch instead of simply halting your spade. (Large rocks are a problem no matter what digging technique you are using.)

Of course, you have to dig the ditch.

Take a wheelbarrow, child's wagon, or some other vehicle to convey the dirt from the ditch to the garden site. If nothing else is available, an old blanket can be used, but make sure you don't load it so heavily with soil that it cannot subsequently be moved. Station your receptacle at one of the narrow ends of the plot—or just at one side if the plot is to be square or circular. Dig the ditch next to the wheelbarrow, tossing all the soil from the ditch into the barrow. You can tell when you have dug enough of a ditch when the wheelbarrow seems to be full of soil. The ditch should be just as deep as the length of the blade of your spade. I prefer to use one of the long, narrow spades, so that I dig deeper. In the glacial-scraped Northeast, I often find that I am reaching into the top of the subsoil, the distinctly yellowish soil that lies under the brown or black topsoil. Most gardening experts tell you only to loosen the subsoil, not to dig into it; alternatively, you can pile the subsoil in a separate place so that it can be replaced below the turned-over topsoil. I am not convinced that this is necessary unless you are digging deep into the subsoil. The inch or two that my long spade penetrates does not disturb the overall soil structure enough to cause me any concern. So I just dig the ditch and toss anything I can reach with the length of my spade into the wheelbarrow.

After the ditch is dug, the hardest part of the job is over. Now you have a cliff from which you can dig clumps with little or no difficulty. Dig along the garden-side wall of the ditch, and throw the spadefuls of soil into the ditch that you dug first. Tossing them will break them up fairly well in good garden soil, but you may also have to hit some of them with the back of your spade to eliminate clods. In clayey soil, you probably will have to hit every spadeful after you toss it into the ditch.

As you advance along the digging face from one end of the ditch to the other, you are creating a new ditch. As the garden is dug, the aim is to move the ditch through the garden from one side to another. You stand on the undug side and dig into the wall of the ditch; in the ditch is a mound of dug soil.

This mound is likely to be 3 to 5 inches higher than the soil outside the garden. That is because the mound is not compacted, but the soil around it has been jammed down. Keep the dug part of the garden that way. Do not walk on the mound at all; stay on your side of the ditch. The uncompacted nature of the soil that has been physically moved, not just turned over, is the second great advantage of this digging method. (The first, of course, is that the method is easier than other ways to dig.)

Eventually you will reach the end of the area that you want the garden to occupy. When that happens, you will still have a ditch, but you also will have a wheelbarrow, wagon, or blanket full of soil. Now is the time to take the reserved soil from the first ditch you dug to the remaining ditch. Use that soil to fill the ditch.

I always find that I have more of a ditch at the end of the operation than I do soil to fill it. No problem. There is a large mound of soil where the garden will be. I fill the ditch as best I can, then when I am hoeing and raking the soil, I finish the job of making the whole thing fairly level. The final result is a mound of soil that is not quite so high as it was, but that is still clearly noncompacted soil. If you are not going to raise the bed, this soil, with suitable additives, will be the soil in which you will plant the herbs. If you are going to raise the bed, this soil is the base area where your herb's roots will take their sustenance year after year. In either case, you'll want to improve it for the best possible healthy crop. On the other hand, if you have dug in the turf that was there in the beginning, the only thing you really need to add is already there—organic matter.

Amendments

While this is a "no-work" herb garden after it is prepared, if you have just completed digging, you know that it is not "no work" in the beginning. If you are truly committed to a "no-work" approach, you can quit work after you finish digging. The herbs will survive in most soils. But if you want to have them thrive instead of merely survive, you need to amend the soil.

If you are going to raise the bed, the amendments should be added in two steps: one before you raise the bed and the other afterward. If the bed is not raised, putting amendments in the soil can be a one-step operation. This is because the best soil needs to be at the top, so that the plants have a lot of nutrients when they are young and have small root systems, and because the nutrients at the top will gradually wash down toward the lower soil levels.

The main thing to add to the lower level of soil in a raised bed is organic matter. In addition to or instead of dug-in turf, the most effective and least expensive way to do this is by adding compost (discussed at length right after this section), but if you do not have compost, manure is a good substitute. Unless the garden is going to be fallow over a winter, the manure should be old—"well rotted" as garden books always say. In the city and even in the suburbs, however, it is often difficult to find a supply of well-rotted manure, but every garden store (and many supermarkets) sell dried or composted manure in 20-pound or 40-pound bags. Either dried or composted manure may be used, but the dried manure is actually more nutritious, while the composted manure is really compost, a better source of organic matter. Thus, if you find only dried manure in your local sources, you may want to supplement it with some other form of organic material (such as chopped-up leaves). If you find only composted manure, it needs no supplement, but you will need more of it to get any real benefit than you would dried manure.

For a perennial garden that uses no artificial fertilizers, use about twice as much dried manure as recommended on the back of the bag and about *four times* as much composted manure as the directions say. The directions were written by someone who assumed that you would add chemicals to the soil, something I prefer not to assume.

There are many reasons for not using artificial fertilizers, but the most important one for this garden plan is that you are not going to dig it up again, and you are not going to want to tend to it every year. Artificial fertilizers do not provide the lasting benefits that naturally decaying materials do.

In addition to adding compost and/or manure, you may want to improve the lower layer in other ways as well. My soil, for example, tends to be deficient in phosphorus, which is, after nitrogen, the element most apt to be in short supply in the soil. The best amendment for correcting that deficiency is crudely ground phosphate rock. For many years phosphate rock was one of the principal fertilizers on earth, but it now is sadly neglected in favor of treated forms of phosphate, such as superphosphate. The key factor, however, is that rocks last and chemicals don't. Superphosphate provides a quick jolt, but phosphate rock slowly decomposes over the years, providing a steady supply of this vital nutrient.

Fertilizer packages are marked with three numbers that represent the amount of the three vital elements that a plant needs to grow. For example, artificial garden fertilizer is often marked 10-10-10, which means that it contains 10 percent each of nitrogen, potassium (also known to gardeners as potash), and phosphorus. Potassium, however, is also available in rock form as either granite dust or greensand. If you can find either of these rock powders (not easily come by, in my neighborhood at least), they should be added to the lower layer along with the compost, manure, and rock phosphate. If you can't find one of them, you will have to count on potassium trickling down from the upper level.

Many soils also need lime—not as a plant nutrient, but to make the nutrients in the soil available to plants. Gardeners' lime—not to be confused with slaked lime—is used to make soil less acid. Herbs, like garden vegetables, prefer a soil that is neither very acid or very alkaline. In areas that get reasonable amounts of rain, soil tends to become acid. The Mediterranean homeland of the common perennial herbs is an area that has moderate rainfall, producing a soil that is near neutral. Thus, if you are in the eastern part of the United States or in a rainy part of the West, you probably need to add lime to the soil. (Inexpensive soil-test kits can help you determine what your needs are.) Futhermore, compost is slightly acid, so it furthers the need for lime in the soil. In dry regions, where the soil is already too alkaline, compost alone is usually the best way to bring the soil into balance. (Sulfur can be used in the case of extremely alkaline soils.)

This completes the amendments that are needed for the lower layer of soil. With one exception—lime—they are required for the top layer as well. The reason that lime may be an exception is that you may want to use wood ashes instead of lime in the top layer. Wood ashes also make soils less acid, and they contain valuable nutrients that lime does not. The top layer may also be enriched with other, more expensive, organic fertilizers. My favorite, for its high nitrogen content, is cottonseed meal. Cottonseed meal is acidic, however, so you need to add extra lime or wood ashes along with it in a herb garden. Cottonseed meal is also useful for making alkaline soils more acidic.

Of course, if you have planned a raised garden, you can substitute wood ashes for lime and also enrich the soil with cottonseed meal in the single layer you will be using. The reason for not putting wood ashes in the lower layer is that the nutrients in ashes are water soluble; they quickly end up in the subsoil—where they do little good. Wood ashes should always be applied to the upper part of the soil (while the other fertilizers can and should be worked in to a reasonable depth), and they should be applied only a short time before plants will be there to use them. If you start a garden in fall, save your wood ashes from a fireplace or stove over the winter, then apply to the soil surface and rake in just before spring planting. If you have no source for wood ashes, a more expensive treatment would be to use a combination of lime and bonemeal, since bonemeal supplies some of the same nutrients that wood ashes supply.

Except for the wood ashes, the organic nutrients can all be added to the soil in the fall for spring planting. Or, if you are willing to let a garden go unplanted for a season—which would drive me crazy—you can prepare the soil in the spring and plant in the early fall. Planting in the fall does have the advantage of getting the plants off to a start when the weather is cool and the sunlight less direct. In some ways, the best of all possible worlds is to prepare the soil *and* plant in the fall. If you do that, however, you must add some quicker-acting fertilizer to the area around each plant. You can use an inorganic 5-10-5 fertilizer, for example. If you are a true organic gardener, however, you will stick to cottonseed meal, bonemeal, dried blood, and fish-soil emulsion to get the plants off to a good start. When the amendments to the soil begin to work, the following spring, you won't have to fertilize again.

Compost

I keep promising to say something about compost, and now seems to be the best time. Compost is largely a combination of waste *and* time, but it is not a waste *of* time, since it is the best all-around soil amendment for any kind of garden. Compost is formed mainly from dead plants, but it may also contain soil, manure, eggshells, unwanted fish, newspapers, and various rock powders. The more different things that go into compost, as long as the materials are compostable, the better the compost is. Basically, any organic material is "compostable" (that is, anything that was at sometime alive), but some materials break down so slowly that they are not worth dealing with. Other materials, especially fats and animal flesh or bones, attract pests that will be unwanted visitors to the compost pile. When soil or rock powders are added to compost, even though they are not, strictly speaking, organic, they become incorporated into the compost, so they can be considered compostable.

The kinds of things that are *not* compostable are rocks, metals, plastics, glass, and chemicals. Sometimes the addition of certain chemicals can make an otherwise compostable substance into one that should be kept out of compost; for example, while ordinary newspaper is a satisfactory ingredient for compost, the chemicals used in colored dyes are not good for compost, so colored inserts in magazines or the Sunday papers are not considered compostable.

Compost is made in a "pile" or "heap." If you are old enough to remember the World War II comic-book character, The Heap, then you remember a creature whose creator was undoubtedly inspired by a compost pile. While there are methods called "sheet composting," the fundamental way of making compost requires a large amount of organic material in one, fairly compact place. One of the main reasons for this is that part of the composting process involves the production of heat by microorganisms and the retention of that heat in the compost. If compostable materials are merely spread around or do not have a compact arrangement, not enough heat is produced at any one place, and the heat that is produced tends to leave the scene. With this consideration in mind, one of the first steps in preparing compost is to find a place where you can stack the materials at least 3 or 4 feet high with a base 5 or 6 feet in diameter. Although it is possible to do this without any method of retaining the walls of the heap in one place, it is far better to make the compost in an enclosure.

Like the comic book character, The Heap, the compost heap is a living creature. Compost (more accurately, the microorganisms that turn organic matter into compost) needs to breathe. (This is the common, *aerobic* method of composting. While compost can be made using organisms that are *anaerobic*, which means that they do not use oxygen for respiration, such methods are avoided by the gardener; one reason is that anaerobic composting is likely to produce noxious smells.)

There are a number of ways to get air into the compost. For one thing, if the compost is rough and not compacted, and not too wet, some air will get in through the spaces between bits of waste. This effect can be multiplied by making sure that the bottom layer of the pile is made from quite rough organic materials—corn stalks, for instance, or even small twigs.

If a retaining wall is built, it should be one that lets the air through. Many people use wire fences as a retaining material. Others build walls with slats. I use concrete blocks placed on their sides so that air comes through the three holes in each block and also through the empty space where two blocks come together. You can also purchase composting bins made of metal or plastic, with many perforations in their sides.

Even though there is provision for air from the bottom (from the rough first layer) and through the sides, the pile will be further helped if there are air holes leading into the interior. Some people build the pile with long sticks, like tomato stakes, in the pile. When the pile is high enough, the sticks are removed, leaving air holes. Other people poke holes in the pile with a stick or hoe handle after the pile is built. I don't do either of these because I seldom build a compost heap all at one time. Instead, I am continually adding grass clippings, or leaves, or plants that have outlived their usefulness.

Because my compost piles do not get a lot of air, they take longer to turn into compost. But I can wait.

Since the compost pile is alive, it needs water as well as air. If you build a compost pile all at once, you can add water to each layer that is added. If each layer is about as wet as a damp sponge, the piles as a whole will start off with the right amount of water. You can continue this practice as you add layers.

The word *layer* is used advisedly. As noted, the more different things that go into compost the better. It is not practical, when building a compost pile, to keep all the ingredients mixed as you go along. On the other hand, if you put all the grass in one place and all the leaves in another, you will have to wait several years for your compost. The solution is to use 3- to 6-inch-thick layers of each material. This provides enough mixing at first. If you later "turn" the pile (more on that soon), the layers will be lost, but the mix will be improved. The main purpose of beginning with layers is to get a good mix without having to stir up the whole pile. (Some commercial composting devices can be rotated, which provides a better stirring than can be accomplished with a pile set on the ground.)

Now let's see. You have a damp pile that the air can get into. It was built in layers, so it is partially mixed. At this point you can go away for a year or more. When you come back, the inner and lower part of the pile will be compost, while the outer part will be material that can be used to rebuild the pile. Some years when I am busy with a lot of other things, that's just what I do.

I can get more compost—and you *always* need more compost than you have—by "turning" the pile once, twice, or even more over the summer. I put *turning* in quotes because you don't just turn the pile over, unless you have a rotating bin. Instead, you take off all the outside material, which is still pretty much in the same condition that it was when you put it in. Pile that off to one side. Then take off the material that looks as if it is turning brown and changing into compost, but which you still recognize as the original material. Pile that somewhere off to another side. Finally, take out the rest, which ought to be rough compost; that is, compost in places, a brown material that looks a lot like rich garden soil, and some parts that are only partly composted. Make that your third pile.

Now rebuild the heap, putting the first pile (which was on the outside before) in the middle; the second pile back where it was; and the third pile on the outside. As you do this, again water each layer so that the whole pile stays about as wet as a damp sponge. When you next get several hours to do this sort of thing, repeat the process. Eventually—but much sooner than if you had not turned the pile—the whole pile will be pure compost, except possibly for a few tough stalks that you can pick out to toss in the next compost heap. People who "turn" their compost heaps every two or three days can make a whole pile of compost in three or four weeks. I make one pile a year, most years.

Compost making can also be speeded up by shredding the material with a shredding machine before it is put into the pile. The smaller pieces let more air in, retain the water better, and turn to compost much sooner. For some purposes, compost not made with a shredder must be sifted through a screen with about a ¼-inch mesh. Otherwise, there will be various bits of wood and other materials in it that have not composted completely.

PLANTING THE GARDEN

Now that you have selected the plants you are going to grow, found a place for your garden, and prepared the soil, you are ready to plant the herbs. There are a number of important considerations here. Luckily, if you do it the no-work way, you merely need to consider them; there is little or no active involvement except for the actual planting.

On the other hand, you may need to consider options that require a little more work, and maybe even put those options into practice. One possible reason is money or the lack of it. This is to be a practical garden; for many people an inexpensive garden that is a bit more work is more practical than an expensive garden that does not involve much labor. There is a scale that stretches from work to cost. The far end of the scale is someone who has hired a gardener, while the close end (closer to me, at least) is someone who has no money, but plenty of time. Most of us are somewhere in between, so I'll lay out several in-between options.

Plants or Seeds?

Herbs are "flowering plants," which means that most of them produce seeds all the time and all of them produce seeds some of the time. Not all the seeds breed true, however. If you want a particular cultivar (that's plant talk for variety or type) of sage, for instance, you are unlikely to get it from seeds. Furthermore, many herbs grow so slowly that you might have to wait until the second year after planting even to consider harvest. Also, for some herbs, such as bay, seeds are rarely available. Finally, one of the most desirable of herbs, tarragon, almost never produces seeds. (There is a form of tarragon, known as Russian tarragon, that produces seeds, but it fails to produce tarragon flavor, so it's no good for cooking purposes. Since tarragon has little to recommend it as a landscape element, tarragon grown from seeds is worthless.)

Of the more common perennial herbs, the best bets for growing from seed are chamomile, lemon balm, lovage, oregano, rosemary, sage, thyme, and winter savory. There are problems with all of them, however. I have grown chamomile from seed sown directly in the garden. It grew, but germinated poorly. I have also grown thyme from seed, and I had to wait a long time before I had much of a plant. It was not until the third year that I could harvest as much as I wanted without worrying about killing the plant.

I have not tried the others, but those who have, report that oregano, rosemary, sage, and winter savory are all about as slow as thyme, with rosemary the slowest. Lovage, it is said, can be planted by laying the seeds on the soil in the late fall, where they will germinate in the spring. Since lovage seeds are very small, and since one probably does not want more than one lovage plant (they are among the largest of herbs), a lot of thinning is necessary in the spring.

Actually, the only thing that growing from seed has going for it is that it is fairly inexpensive if you want a lot of a particular herb. For the practical herb gardener, however, a single plant of most of the perennial herbs will suffice. The exceptions among the perennials, plants that are needed in larger quantities, are chamomile, chives, Egyptian onions, and mint, of which only chamomile is likely to be available as seeds.

If you have no other source of chamomile—which is quite likely—you should try growing it from seeds. Next time I start a patch of chamomile, which will be soon—my present batch almost all died out from frost and weeds—I will change my method. Instead of planting the chamomile directly in the soil, I will start it in the house in starting soil in flats. Starting soil is what its name suggests—sterilized, lightweight soil especially prepared for starting needs. Flats are just shallow boxes with some drainage. I always use half-gallon milk cartons cut in half lengthwise, with a few cuts in the bottom for drainage.

To start seed in flats, fill the flats with soil to a depth of at least an inch. Place individual seeds an inch or so apart, following the directions on the packet. Thoroughly wet the soil. Place each flat in a plastic bag that has a small hole cut in it, and tie up the end of the bag. The hole permits some air exchange but prevents the water from evaporating too fast. Place the bags out of direct sunlight for a week or two until the seeds begin to germinate. You should see tiny plants emerging from the soil.

When the plants first start to pop up, remove the flat from the bag, and place the flat in a well-lighted, draft-free window or under fluorescent lights. The first leaves of most plants are called seed leaves; they generally do not resemble the leaves of the adult plants. When two or three of the true leaves have emerged, transplant the seedlings to individual pots. For the herbs discussed here, the best time to start seeds would be about six to eight weeks before the last frost date. Set them out after all danger of frost has past. If the herbs are still quite tiny, however, you may want to keep them indoors for quite a bit longer, perhaps even until toward the end of summer, after the highest temperatures have passed. Then they should be set out six to eight weeks before the first frost.

In general, however, if you want to minimize work and maximize chances of success, you are better off starting with small plants if these are available in your locality. If not, many herbs can be bought as plants from seed catalogs, even from companies that do not specialize in herbs. Most herbs sold in garden stores come in small pots. Herbs from seed catalogs are apt to be bare-rooted and in damp plastic bags when they arrive. I think that most herbs make the transition from store to garden better in the small pots, but sometimes the most raggedly-looking, naked plant in a plastic bag will thrive.

Vegetative Reproduction

There is a way to acquire the herbs for your garden that is even less expensive than starting seeds and is also much less work. But there is a catch; there is no such thing as a completely free lunch. This *almost* free lunch requires that you know someone who already has a herb garden with the herbs you desire. Also, this method is more complicated for some herbs that it is for others. Nevertheless, if you have found the necessary herb gardener, and if the gardener is willing to cooperate (which almost all are), you have it made.

The method is based on the fact that most plants reproduce themselves from small pieces of themselves; among the higher animals, this is true largely of starfish and some worms. Even giant trees, however, can be reproduced from a branch or even a leaf. Because this method of reproduction is common among plants and uncommon among higher animals, the method is called *vegetative reproduction*.

If you grow flowers or potatoes, you are familiar with one form of vegetative reproduction—growth from bulbs or tubers. Similarly, if you grow fruit trees, you may know another form—growth from branches or twigs. Plants may also be grown from leaves or from ordinary roots. All they need is some encouragement. Different methods are used for different types of herbs, however.

Bay. Since I am discussing these in alphabetical order, I am starting with one of the hardest to grow vegetatively. It is possible to start a bay plant by cutting a stem from the tree and keeping the stem in water. You will have a slightly better chance if you dip the end of the stem in a plant growth hormone. Hormones especially made for starting plants are available in most garden stores and through some seed catalogs. The problem is that the bay is normally a slow grower, and it is just as slow in starting new roots. You might want to try it anyway.

The best method is to place the bay twig in perlite, an absorbent medium that is also available in garden stores. Trim the leaves from the end of the twig that is going into the perlite, but keep the rest of the leaves. Dampen the stem end with water, and then dip it into the plant hormone. Keep the twig in damp perlite in a window. It is a good idea to put a plastic bag (with the usual small hole cut in it) over the whole plant and pot to keep the moisture in. Be sure to tie the bag tightly.

If you are lucky, after about a year, the roots will have begun to form, and you can transplant the new little bay tree to a pot. If you are unlucky, the leaves will eventually dry on the twig and the chances of starting a tree this time are gone. You can increase your chance of success by trying to start more than one bay tree at a time (if your gardening friend has a big-enough bay to spare several twigs).

It will be hard to tell if you have succeeded without taking the twig out of the perlite, which can damage small roots. As long as the leaves stay green, however, you have a chance of success. Probably the best thing to do is to wait until there is some small sign of growth (such as a new bud) before inspecting the possible roots. All in all, starting a bay tree is so chancy that you might want to wait until you can buy a small plant from someone else. On the other hand, starting a bay tree *is* something of an adventure.

Chamomile. It is said that the best way to obtain chamomile is to start it vegetatively, but I have never found anyone else who grew it from whom I could "borrow" a hunk or two of plant. The same method, however, can be used to increase your own stock of chamomile. The method is called *root division* or simply *division*. The idea is to break the plant in two so that each half has roots, stems, and leaves. When replanted, each of the halves will grow into a new plant. This is a much easier method than starting a cutting, as can be done with bay, because you can plant the divisions directly (with no long, watchful time in the house). It is easy to see why some plants, such as the bay, are not susceptible to root division—you would have to cut the single stem in half. Other plants, such as chamomile, have multiple stems that can be separated from each other along with part of the roots. There is no trick to root division. If the halves are planted again at the same depth as the "mother" plant, the "daughters" will grow almost as if nothing had happened to them. You should, however, make root divisions in the spring or in the early fall so that the "daughters" have a chance to develop full strength before facing the rigors of a hot summer or freezing winter.

Chives. Chives *multiply*. That is, each year there are new plants growing next to the old ones. This habit eventually results in crowded conditions that are not good for the crop. Every two or three years a careful gardener should dig up all the chives and replant just the bulbs desired, at least an inch or two apart. The remaining bulbs can then be used by another gardener to start his or her own patch of chives.

Comfrey. Comfrey can also be grown from root divisions, but it is such a vigorous plant that it also can be grown from *root cuttings*. Root cuttings are just bits or pieces of root that have no stems or leaves attached. For comfrey (and for most plants that grow from root cuttings), the pieces of root are buried horizontally a couple of inches deep in the soil. After a few weeks, they should send up new stems.

Egyptian Onions. Egyptian onions produce small growths called bulbils, or bulblets, at the tops of their stems. These may be planted an inch or so deep in the soil, where they will produce new plants. Egyptian onions also multiply by themselves. Each year there will be a somewhat larger cluster of bulbs, essentially individual plants, growing close together. You can lift the whole cluster and divide it the way you would a root division.

Lemon Balm. While lemon balm can be grown from seed, from stem cuttings taken in the spring or summer, and from root divisions taken in the early spring, it hardly seems worthwhile to bother. Lemon balm is related to the mints, and like them it grows new plants all over the garden if it is not contained. In fact, I find lemon balm somewhat more troublesome than true mints, for the lemon balm "babies" are apt to appear 10 feet or more away from the parent plant. Therefore, the best way to grow lemon balm vegetatively is to dig up one of the babies and replant it where you would like it to be. Of course, if your friend the gardener has adequately contained the original lemon balm, you may be forced to obtain a stem cutting or to wait until the gardener makes a root division.

Lovage. Lovage can be started from root divisions as well as from seeds.

Mint. As noted above, mint produces many new plants every year, often where they are not wanted. Also like lemon balm, mints can be grown from root divisions or stem cuttings.

Oregano. Many plants require root division every two or three years to keep them healthy; oregano is one of them. If the plant is not divided, the roots get all tangled and in the way of each other. Therefore, if you have an oregano plant, it is likely that you will divide it from time to time, and you may wonder what to do with the other half. (One-half is replanted in the same spot, with its roots untangled.) As a result, it is fairly easy to obtain an oregano plant from anyone who grows the herb if you wait until the year of division. Furthermore, if oregano is not contained, as a member of the mint family it produces unwanted volunteers that need to be dug out of the garden and disposed of somehow.

Rosemary. For the most part, rosemary is grown from stem cuttings, following the same procedure used for bay that is outlined above. Instead of waiting a year, however, you usually need to wait only a few weeks before signs of new growth begin (and they are much more certain to begin with rosemary than with bay). There is another method of vegetative propagation that can also be used with rosemary. If one of the branches is pinned to the soil with a U-shaped piece of wire or even a bent twig, the branch will form roots at the place it is pinned to the soil. When that happens, the branch may be cut between the pinned-down place and the parent plant, producing a new plant that can later be transplanted to any desirable location (later because it should have a few weeks to develop before transplanting). This method of vegetative reproduction is called *layering*, for reasons that I have never been able to determine.

Sage. Root cuttings are the traditional way to propagate sage, although layering, described above, also works.

Tarragon. Like oregano, tarragon needs to be divided every two or three years for good health, and one half of the division can be moved to another garden to form a new plant. Unlike oregano, tarragon is not likely to grow satellite plants very far from the main one.

Thyme. Although there are many varieties of thyme, they all grow easily from root divisions or from stem cuttings. Some varieties of low-growing thyme propagate themselves along cracks between rocks, forming an aromatic mat over the rocks. Normally, one thinks of the species called mother-of-thyme as spreading in that way, but some varieties of lemon thyme will do the same. The most common type of thyme grown for cooking purposes, known as common thyme or garden thyme, grows quite woody as the plant grows older. Since you want freshly growing tips of thyme for cooking, it is best to start common thyme ever two or three years from stem cuttings, and replace the old plant with a new one.

Winter Savory. Winter savory is much like oregano in its growth habits, although it looks a lot like common thyme. It should be divided every two or three years and can be grown from root divisions. It also grows readily from stem cuttings and produces offspring if it is not contained. Actually, it is more aggressive than oregano and almost as aggressive as lemon balm.

If you know someone who grows one or more of the perennial herbs, it should be possible to obtain a stem, root, root division, or unwanted plant with no difficulty. Periodically, most people who grow herbs want to dispose of extra chives, Egyptian onions, lemon balm, mint, oregano, tarragon, and winter savory. If they are sensitive souls, they will not want to dump their root divisions or "babies" in the compost heap. They will want to find a nice home for the plants. You only need to make it clear that you will provide such a home, and you, too, may soon find yourself with more plants than you want.

Buying Herbs

I prefer to save time and effort by buying small potted herbs at local garden stores. However, I live in a part of the country where such herbs are readily available. By shopping around, I can often find a herb I want for as little as 69¢, although some of the tonier establishments charge as much as $2 a herb for plants that are only slightly larger than the inexpensive ones I buy. Besides, I like to shop around for plants; I find garden stores very pleasant places to be.

Vegetative reproduction and purchasing plants share one very important benefit over starting plants from seeds. You can be sure of what kind of plant you are getting. Not only do seeds often fail to breed true, but also one man's oregano is another man's marjoram. The plants you find for oregano, tarragon, and chamomile are particularly susceptible to various interpretations. Tasteless tarragon was discussed in the section on growing from seed. Before you buy a tarragon plant you should snip off a bit of leaf and taste it. If the leaf does not have a pronounced licoricelike flavor, pass the plant by (and go to another store).

Chamomile comes in two unrelated species, one that grows to a height of about 3 inches for the most part and one that commonly grows to be about a foot high. While both species of chamomile have similar flavors, you should look for the one that fits into your garden plans. A small pot plant may not indicate much about its eventual height. The short-growing form is the perennial, and its stem should lie flat on the ground. The label should say "Roman chamomile" or "true chamomile." The tall-growing form is the annual, and its stem should be erect. The label should say "German chamomile."

Oregano is the toughest case of all, because oregano varies from plant to plant so much. There need be no mislabeling to cause confusion. For example, for years I have grown an oregano that has leaves on short stems. I am very happy with its flavor, which is more akin to majoram than it is to the dried oregano commonly available in stores. A friend of mine who also grows herbs, however, failed to recognize either the plant or the flavor as oregano. Shortly after my friend commented on my unusual variety of oregano, my wife happened to be in a garden store that was having a herb sale, so she bought several plants. One was oregano, but this oregano has leaves on which the stems are so short they do not seem to be there at all; the color of its leaves is much more bronze than the bright green of my original oregano; and the flavor leans heavily toward the taste I grew to love when I was adding extra oregano to my pizza in college days. I am now pleased to grow both varieties of oregano.

Oregano is but the most dramatic case of a general tendency of both perennial and many annual herbs—the tendency to vary. The reason is that herbs are not, for the most part, bred into particular varieties by seed companies and research labs. There's not enough money in it. I find this lack of attention to my favorite plants quite pleasant. It means that the herbs are closer to nature than the well-known, rock-hard tomatoes bred for shipping or the tasteless, red Delicious apple. The side effect, however, is that even the most experienced herb gardener needs to taste and to look very closely when buying new herbs (or even when obtaining root divisions or cuttings from a friend).

The Actual Planting

Once you have your herbs (whether as a result of starting seeds, buying plants, or obtaining divisions or cuttings), and once you have prepared the soil completely, the actual planting is quite simple. You can, for the most part, simply dig a hole and put the herb into it, keeping the roots spread out as much as possible and keeping the point at which the roots and stem meet at ground level. If you like, you can put some bonemeal and compost at the base of the hole, covering the added nutrients with a half-inch or so of soil. This will get the herb off to a better start, but it is not necessary for perennial herbs in well-prepared garden soil. This practice makes much more sense for annual plants, especially those that need to grow enough to produce seeds or fruit in abundance within the single growing season allotted to the plants.

After all the herbs are in the ground, it is important to water the entire garden quite thoroughly. Roots need the water in the beginning until they get in touch with the soil around them. Watering also helps settle the soil around the roots. Finally, the plants may tend to wilt a bit, and water on the leaves as well as on the soil helps to reduce this wilting, which is unhealthy for the newly planted herbs.

Another way to reduce wilting is to plant late in the afternoon, so the plants have a chance to recover overnight before the sun hits them. Cloudy days are better for planting than sunny ones for the same reason. The best time to plant is on a cloudy day when rain is forecast.

The problems with planting herbs have little to do with the actual plants; instead you should be concerned about where the herbs will be planted and whether or not they need to be contained in some way. Some herbs, such as chamomile or low-growing thymes, may be encouraged to spread, but others, especially the members of the mint family, probably will need to be discouraged from moving out into new quarters each year.

I cannot give you absolute rules to follow about placing herbs; much depends on the effect you want to achieve. For most of the perennial herbs, the most important thing is to give each plant enough room to grow. Here is a suggested spacing.

1 or More Feet Apart. Bay, comfrey, lemon balm, lovage, oregano, sage, tarragon, common thyme, winter savory.

2 to 4 Inches Apart. Chamomile, chives, Egyptian onions, mint, creeping thymes.

This is a very rough guide, of course, because herbs are often planted for effect as well as for their benefits as flavors, teas, or scents. If you want to grow common thyme as a mass or as a border, for example, closer spacing, perhaps even less than a foot apart, may be desired. On the other hand, if you want a specimen plant of thyme to use primarily for its leaves as a flavoring, it should be more than a foot from its nearest neighbor for best growth.

A few of the herbs can grow quite large. Lovage is probably the champion in northern climates, but rosemary can spread for several feet in diameter when it can be grown year-round in the ground in southern parts of the country. Also, in the south a bay tree is really a tree and can be as much as 60 feet high when conditions are right, but a container-grown bay is only a shrub, reaching 5 or 6 feet after many years. Comfrey can easily spread to a diameter of 3 feet or more in any climate. Not only does it need room for its own sake, but also comfrey should not be very close to a neighbor for another reason. If you want to be able to find that neighbor when you are looking for a snip to add to your omelette, you will have to search for it under the broad leaves of the comfrey plant.

In general, with the exception of chamomile, some thymes, lovage, and bay, the herbs discussed here are all about the same height, something between 1 and 2 feet, in northern climates. (In the south, rosemary can grow to about 5 feet and the bay, as noted, becomes a tree.) Perennial chamomile and creeping thyme grow only a few inches in height, and can be used for lawns, just as grass is. Lovage and potted bay are often around 4 feet in height.

All herbs need a fair amount of sunlight, but if you must plant them in a place that doesn't get full sunlight all day, the chances are that some parts of that place get more sunlight than the others. The herbs that can thrive best in partial shade include lovage, comfrey, parsley, and the mints.

Now you have a number of criteria that should be used in planning where to set out the herbs in your garden.

For the plainest type of no-work kitchen garden, the one that is about the size of a gravesite, the one that contains, say, just chives and a single plant each of oregano, sage, tarragon, and thyme, the easiest plan is to put a clump of chives and a single specimen of every other plant just 1½ or 2 feet apart in a single line. In this case, the plants are all about the same size and color is not a factor

Oregano and tarragon may grow somewhat taller than sage or thyme, so you may wish to put the taller plants in the middle. If the chives are not treated as a clump, spaced the same as the other plants, they can be put in a border, in which case you plant each single bulb a couple of inches from its neighbor in a row along one or more sides of the garden. Allow space for the chives to form a border at least 6 inches wide, for they spread rapidly from year to year.

For a garden that contains more plants, you need to work out a more complex design, of course. One possibility for people who have perennial flower gardens is to integrate the herbs into the flowers. This means still more complicated planning, but the effects can be quite striking. But that is on the level of serious gardening, not no-work gardening.

Aside from determining where you will place the plants, there is one other important consideration for certain of the herbs. Mention has been made several times of containing certain aggressive plants. You have to do something about this if you want the garden to stay the same as you originally planned it. One way to do this is to pull out ruthlessly the unwanted volunteers each year. This is a lot of unnecessary work if the plants are properly contained when they are first planted.

The way to contain plants is to make a barrier for their roots. Herbs of the mint family propage by sending out long roots underground, from which new plants grow at intervals. In some cases, the new plants can be as much as 10 feet from the original plant. Stop the roots and you stop the volunteers. Any barrier that is deep enough in the ground and permanent will do. The best one I ever found was a crock that I had formerly used for making dill pickles and sauerkraut. I had left it outside on a cold night with a small amount of water in the bottom. When the water froze, the bottom of the crock fell out. Now I had a glazed, straight-sided cylinder that was about a foot in diameter and about a foot and a half high. I buried it in the herb garden with its rim just above ground level, and an oregano plant has thrived in it for years. (I do miss the crock, however; I am not suggesting this as a general plan to follow, but rather as an example of how you can sometimes find a useful function in the garden for something that has outlived its usefulness elsewhere.)

The nearest thing to my broken crock that is easily available and that does the job is an 18-inch drainage tile, the kind that does *not* have holes in the sides. Not only do such tiles contain the herb, but also they produce very attractive round groups of plants that add to the visual beauty of the garden. While a shorter tile, say a foot in length, might do the job, I think you will be safer with the 18-inch length, especially since shorter tiles are apt to be smaller in diameter. Plastic tiles are just as good as glazed pottery, and considerably less expensive.

The herbs that desperately *need* to be contained are the mints, lemon balm, oregano, and winter savory. Other herbs that are convenient to contain are clumps of chives, comfrey, lovage (in a somewhat larger container than a tile), and tarragon. This will prevent spreading and make for easier care of the plants, as well as a neater appearance. Of course, this list refers to containers that are open at the bottom and sunk in the ground. Containers that can be placed on the ground and carried inside for the winter may need to be used for bay or rosemary in colder climates. If most of the plants are contained in sunken containers, you may want to finish off the job by putting all of them in containers, since the containers help keep some weeds out as well as keeping the herbs in.

ELIMINATING CARE

So far, you probably think that a no-work herb garden is mainly a lot of hard work. There is one more piece of work to do to reach the no-work stage, in fact, although not necessarily a big or difficult task. One spring spent getting properly organized should mean many years of simply enjoying the garden. Now that the plants are in the ground, you are almost organized. If you stop at this point, you will have a herb garden that needs frequent weeding and, at times, frequent watering. Since that will continue year after year, while the initial setting up is done only once, it is essential to take steps to prevent the necessity of weeding and watering. Fortunately, the same step prevents both.

What you need to do is to *mulch* the garden. A mulch is any covering for the garden that prevents weed growth and conserves water. There are a vast number of choices among mulches, although they fall into essentially two categories—organic and inorganic. *Organic* here means the same as it did when we were thinking about fertilizer. An organic mulch was at some time or another alive. While an inorganic mulch may in some way have been alive, events or people have changed it so much that it no longer dissolves into the soil the way that organic mulches may have. For example, plastic is made from hydrocarbons, which in turn may be made from oil or coal, which may once have been the remains of living creatures. By the time the chain stretches from living creatures millions of years ago through a modern chemical factory to your garden, plastic mulches are so far removed from their organic origins that they are considered to be inorganic.

The principal benefit of organic mulches is that over time they decay, producing nutrients for plants and enriching the soil structure. This is an extremely positive benefit for the vegetable garden or for any garden that will be dug up each year and remulched. For a perennial herb garden, however, the essential point of organic mulches implies that new mulch needs to be added every year. If you want the garden to be care-free after it is set up, use inorganic mulches. Inorganic mulches are also less expensive in the long run because you will need to add a layer of an inorganic mulch at least once a year to make up for the part that has decayed.

Now that the basic principles have been set forth, let's look at a list of some of the possible mulches you can use.

Organic. straw, hay, or seaweed; chopped bark or sawdust; cocoa or buckwheat hulls; lawn clippings; or newspapers.

Inorganic. rocks or plastic.

I find that straw is fine for my vegetable garden, although I prefer salt hay (which has no seeds in it that can contribute to the weed population). Salt hay is fairly expensive, however. The problem with straw, hay, and seaweed in the herb garden is that it is not very attractive. No one expects a vegetable garden to look that aesthetic, but herb gardens are traditionally considered to be a contribution to the landscape as well as to flavors, scents, and so forth. If you don't care about looks, a layer several inches thick of stray, hay, or seaweed is a perfectly good mulch, but it needs to be renewed annually.

Chopped bark is attractive and is available at garden stores in several degrees of fineness. It may not require renewing for several years because it decays slowly. The decay process for wood may rob the soil of nitrogen, however, so chopped bark and sawdust both require that you add a high nitrogen fertilizer to the soil each year. Also, sawdust decays faster than bark, and may require more frequent renewal.

Cocoa and buckwheat hulls are about the most attractive of all the organic mulches. They are both expensive, however, and decay rapidly. I have had cocoa hulls disappear completely within a couple of months—so I don't use them anymore. Also, I could not quite get used to the idea that my herb garden smelled like a cup of hot chocolate.

Grass clippings are free for most people. They are high in

nitrogen and quite good for the soil. They have to be renewed frequently, but anyone with a lawn has a good supply of clippings, so renewal is not usually a problem. The main complaint I have about grass clippings is that they do not look very nice. At first, when they are still a pale green, they look fine; but soon they turn an unpleasant shade of brown. They also form mats that look—well, matted.

Newspapers look even worse. Also, newspapers need some other kind of mulch on top of them (grass clippings for example). Otherwise, they will blow away. Newspapers are very good at keeping down weeds. A combination of newspapers topped with an attractive mulch, such as cocoa shells, can save you money. Using the newspapers means that you do not need so thick a layer of the other mulch. Also, I believe that the top layer of mulch does not decay so quickly when it is on a newspaper base. (*Note*: If you use newspapers, avoid the colored supplements, as the dyes used for the color may be harmful to plants.)

Black plastic is sold in garden stores as an inorganic mulch. While it does not contribute to the nutrition of the soil, black plastic has an important role in the vegetable garden. Because it absorbs heat readily, it warms the soil, causing greater growth of plants from tropical climates, such as squash and beans. It is also extremely effective at preventing weeds. Each plant can be planted through a slit or small hole in the plastic; no other plants can emerge. It makes for a very artificial-looking garden, however. Also, although black plastic does not decay, various rips and tears can develop easily, especially if dogs or deer walk on the surface. Finally, plastic needs to be weighted or pinned down at the edges or it will blow away.

I was concerned the first time I used black plastic about the problems that rain would have getting through the plastic. These fears seem to have been groundless. Apparently, the plastic tends to funnel rainwater into the holes from which the desired plants emerge. Other areas of the garden may not get much water, but the needed areas seems to get enough. Once the water is in the ground, of course, the plastic keeps it from evaporating easily.

Although black plastic is sold in strips, you may find it less expensive to use plastic bags that are intended for garbage or for lawn cleanup materials. If such bags have been used to collect leaves, for example, then they may develop a rip or hole. Such a tear may make the bag unsuitable for further use in holding leaves, but it does not interfere with its potential as a mulch.

Clear plastic may also be used as a mulch, but it has no benefits over black plastic and does not provide the warming effect to the soil. Also, it is not usually sold in garden stores, although it may be obtained from hardware stores in various thicknesses.

Rocks are perfectly good mulches. Even though they are not organic, strictly speaking, they can contribute to useful minerals in the soil. They can be chosen to be attractive, and they are the most permanent kind of mulch you can get.

Of course, there are rocks and there are rocks. The most effective kind for keeping down weeds are the small rocks that form a gravel, but gravel usually must be purchased. The free kind are the type I dig up every time I turn over a spadeful of soil. They are mostly too large and often are a particularly unpleasant shade of brown.

For a completely weed-free garden that needs little or no care once it has been set up, rock mulch is the obvious choice. However, the thickness of rocks required to keep the weeds out may be too great for low-growing herbs.

I recommend the following procedure: initially plant the herbs in black plastic weighted down with a mulch of free rocks if they are available. If they are not available, use commercial gravel (or other attractive gravel) as a top layer of mulch. If you have a layer of free rocks, and if they are as unattractive as the ones I dig up, you may want to add a layer of more attractive rocks over them. Because of the plastic base, the rock layers do not have to be deep. A rock mulch should be shallow enough for all herbs but chamomile or creeping thyme (if they are included in your garden); there is no good way to mulch either of these plants. I have not figured out a trick for chamomile that prevents weeding, but creeping thyme grows well in the *cracks* between larger rocks that have been set close together in the ground. The thyme will eventually cover the rocks and look like a carpet of thyme. It will also smother almost all weeds.

In my own garden, I followed the procedure of mulching with a combination of used lawn cleanup bags and free rocks with one slight variation. Since we live near the Atlantic Ocean and visit the beach a few times a year, I have gotten in the habit of picking up attractive beach rocks that are about an inch in diameter. These beach rocks form the top layer of rocks in the garden, forming a most appropriate setting for the herbs, many of which normally grow near the sea in their original habitat. What is more, beach rocks are free. (If you try this, please note that I originally started by picking up much smaller rocks. After a while, I discovered that small rocks do not do the job in the quantities you can normally pick up at the beach. You need just too many of them to make an adequate covering if you are picking them up by hand. Go for the ones from ½ to 2 inches in diameter.)

Over several years, the plastic mulch may deteriorate and a few weeds may come up. But there will not be many weeds, and they will be easily removed.

Watering the Garden

Of course, there is another purpose to the mulch besides preventing weeding. It also reduces the need to water. Most common herbs do not need much water anyway. Often they have small, somewhat glossy leaves, perfectly suited to keeping water from evaporating too fast. Most herbs do better if they dry out from time to time, rather than being waterlogged.

Nevertheless, even with a mulch, if there is a prolonged dry spell the herbs may need watering. Because of herbs' small, somewhat glossy leaves, it is hard to tell when typical perennial herbs are in need of additional water. A good clue, however, is to look at the other plants in the neighborhood that are less well adapted to lack of water. This includes most vegetables and annual flowers, but not large perennial flowers, bushes, or trees, all of which have root systems that go further in search of water than the root systems of most herbs. If the annual plants show signs of wilting, then the herbs probably need water also. When you feel that such a situation occurs, be sure that you water thoroughly. Five or even ten minutes with a hose sprayed over the plants is not likely to be enough. One way to check the amount you have watered is to put a pan of some kind in among the herbs. Then you can watch the water level in the pan as you go along. There should be at least an inch in the pan before you stop.

If you have watered sufficiently, you need not water again for several days or even a week. The exception to this concerns plants in pots (for example bay or rosemary). The potted plants have no mulch for protection and no deep soil in which their roots can take refuge. While potted plants outdoors do not usually need to be watered as often as plants in the house in most weather (not only is there occasional rain, but also the plants will get some water from dew and from the humidity that is generally higher outdoors than in the house), they need much more frequent watering than plants in the ground do. In weather that is very dry and sunny, potted plants outdoors may dry out from the sunlight so much that they should be watered daily. Certainly if you are watering the rest of the herbs once a week, the potted plants should be watered at least twice a week.

There are a number of different theories about what time of the day is best to water. For many people the only really convenient time is late in the afternoon, after they have returned from work. Fortunately, the theory that I hold is that for most situations, that *is* the best time. The reason, of course, is so the water will not evaporate in the hot sun. (I know the sun is hot, since you are in the middle of a dry spell or you would not need to water.) Plants that are susceptible to mildew, such as lilac, might be adversely affected by watering late in the day. Water on the plant's leaves or stems will not evaporate quickly during the night—a good setup for mildew to form. However, I have yet to meet a herb that mildews.

If you let your herbs blossom, instead of cutting them so often that blossoms never quite make it, there is a minor, but real, danger involved in watering herbs in later summer, when the plants are most likely to need it. Many herbs, especially oregano and thyme among the perennials, are extremely attractive to bees and wasps when they are in flower. Watering sometimes angers the insects. I have found it prudent to work my spray slowly toward the plants that are getting the most attention from my chitinous friends. If the insects receive the warning of the sound of falling water as it gradually approaches, most bees and wasps fly off in the other direction. A sudden direct spray makes bees mad—although I have only been stung once in the herb garden, and that was when I moved a timber that had a wasp nest under it. Nevertheless, I often felt under attack while watering until I adopted the gradual approach.

CARE FOR THE CARE-FREE GARDEN

Now you have a garden for which the site is, of course, perfect, the soil prepared for many years of plenitude, the herbs carefully chosen, and a mulch laid down that will enable you to leave the garden alone except for the times that you want to admire it or to pluck a sprig of thyme for a stew. Well, you almost have that. No garden can be completely care-free. I have already mentioned watering in prolonged dry spells. There have been hints that tender herbs (that is, those that cannot stand cold weather) cannot be left outside all year in many climates. There are a few other necessities that are neither costly nor time-consuming.

Even the herbs that are not so tender that they need to be brought in for the winter may require some help to get through that difficult season in northern climates. Remember that the habitat of many of the common herbs was originally the shores of the Mediterranean—hardly the same as the northern Midwest of the United States or even the Atlantic seaboard where I live. While the Mediterranean climate has both wet and dry seasons, it does not have a real temperate-zone winter. Herbs can stand a certain amount of cold weather, snow, and ice, for they have encountered these conditions in their ancestral home. They cannot stand temperatures that are below zero for days at a time combined with ice storms and winds that remove the moisture from the leaves. The worst damage seems to occur in the late winter or early spring, perhaps after a brief warm spell has convinced the plants that winter is over and it is okay to let their guard down.

The remedy for this is to protect the herbs from cold, ice, and wind. There are a number of ways this can be done, but the easiest is simply to cover the plants completely (or so just the tips show) with straw or hay. If this covering is applied properly, the straw or hay will cover the herbs, but will not be heavy enough to press them down or to bend branches. All the herbs should be covered with mulch, but thyme, sage, and oregano seem to be the most sensitive. Mints, comfrey, tarragon, lemon balm, and chives die back in the winter, so they are in less danger. Winter savory and chamomile are hardier than other herbs but can be killed by an unusually severe cold spell.

Ideally, the time to cover the herbs is *after* the ground has frozen. If you cover the herbs too early in the winter, they will not be fully prepared for winter. After the ground has frozen, the mulch will tend to keep it frozen. When it does thaw, it will thaw slowly, and if it refreezes, it will refreeze slowly. The slow freezing or thawing helps prevent the root damage that can be caused by unmulched ground. In extreme cases of quick freezing and thawing, the ground may buckle or heave, exposing the roots to damage from the cold air.

Just as it is important not to spread the winter protection too early, it is even more important not to remove it too soon. Plants are not the only creatures who can be fooled by a warm spell early in the spring. It can get very cold in March, and that is when most damage to the herbs is likely to occur. The end of winter is not obvious from the temperature and the start of spring is not the same on the calendar in different microclimates. While a climate map of the United States will have a single climate zone encompass Sussex County on Long Island, Westchester County (where I live), and

Sullivan County in the Catskill Mountains, the actual climates are very different. Although both Sussex County and Sullivan County are about an hour's drive from my house, when it is spring in Westchester it can still be winter in Sussex or Sullivan.

One way to learn when spring has actually arrived in your own microclimate is to rely on careful records kept from year to year, making some adjustment for the severity of the past winter. This is a lot of trouble. Besides, it doesn't begin to help until you have done it for several years.

A better way to know when winter is over is to find some indicator in the environment. American Indians used to wait to plant corn until the leaves of the oaks were the size of mouse's ears. (I generally avoid getting close enough to mice to determine the size of their ears. Besides, I am reasonably sure that the ears of the field mouse must have been meant, not those of the house mouse. Field mice have bigger ears than house mice, which further complicates the problem.) I have come to depend upon the lilac.

Fortunately, lilacs are ubiquitous in most areas of the United States that have severe winters. Chances are that you can use the same method even if you do not have your own lilac in the yard. Lilacs develop small leaves late in the spring. If conditions are right for the lilacs to be leafing out, then the chances are very good that conditions are right to remove the mulch. If you want to be extra careful, however, you might remove only half of the mulch when the lilac leaves are small, waiting to remove the remainder when the lilac is fully in leaf.

Should it happen that you have no convenient lilac to watch, you should look at other deciduous shrubs or trees, finding a local species that leafs out at the proper time. This may take a couple of years before you are sure, however. For those two years, it would be better to leave the herbs covered until you are quite certain that winter has passed. The herbs will not be hurt if the mulch is thin enough to allow some sunlight to pass through.

Aside from providing a mulch in the winter, there is little that needs to be done annually. Herbs really do need little care.

There is a task that *should* be done every three years, although nothing spectacular goes wrong if you don't do it for a longer period of time. It is called *dividing*, and the concept is explained in the discussion of vegetative propagation. Chives and tarragon especially need to be divided for good health, although comfrey, lovage, oregano, thyme, and winter savory will also do better if lifted from the ground and divided periodically. This is largely because the roots begin to crowd each other, but also because the plants have begun to use up some of the immediate available nutrients in the soil. Most of the plants that can be divided form multiple stems.

A division is made by separating some of the stems and the roots attached to those stems from the rest of the plant. The separation is best made with a sharp knife. A plant can be divided into two plants, or if it is somewhat larger, into three plants. One of the plants is then returned to the old home—but a home that has been furnished in the plant's brief absence with compost, bonemeal, and other nice things. Also, the plant that is returned to the original spot should have its roots untangled as much as possible. Water it well, so the soil can settle and so the rootlets have a chance to penetrate the soil anew. As with all transplants, dividing is best accomplished on a cloudy afternoon, especially when rain is in the offing.

As a practical matter, I always divide chives and tarragon whether they need it or not. As a lazy gardener, I do not divide the others unless they show some signs of ill health, such as poor growth, lack of flowering, yellow- or brown-edged leaves, or lack of resistance to insects.

If you want to expand your garden, you might want to divide more frequently. The divisions that you do not return to from whence they came can be used anywhere you want. Of course, if you need to divide and do not want any more of a particular herb or do not have room for it, the excess root divisions can be added to the compost heap. If you want a supply of a herb dried, the roots can be removed from the divisions, and the whole stems with the leaves attached can be hung in the attic to dry (preferably in upside-down paper bags, to keep the dust off; just poke the cut end of the stem through the bag and tie it with a piece of thread to a rafter or hook).

After the herbs have dried, some people like the looks of the dried whole plants enough that they tie a nice bundle of them to a hook in the kitchen. If that does not suit you, you can remove the leaves and store them in tightly closed jars, although that is a messy job. But it is certainly often more satisfying to give the plants away then to dry them, especially if you give them to someone who has admired your garden or who occasionally bums a herb or two from you for some special recipe.

Chives are unlike the other herbs in this list because they form totally separate plants, not single plants with multiple stems. The new plants are formed next to the old ones, so the effect is the same, however—crowding, especially for the original plants that are now surrounded by their progeny. If the clumps are not divided, the chives get smaller and more grasslike as the years go by. Flowers, too, will be smaller or may not appear at all, which would be a shame because the flowers are one of the nicest sights in the garden. When you divide the chives, dig them all up, replanting about a third of them a couple of inches apart (to form a border) or perhaps an inch apart (in a clump). This leaves you with a great many chives to give away or to throw on the compost heap. There is a third alternative, however; you can chop them and freeze the chopped chives for use in the winter. The frozen chives may also be more than you need, so consider giving some of them away to people who would like to have chives but do not want to grow them.

Sometimes thyme is handled in a different way from root divisions. Thyme has a tendency to become woody over the years. As the thyme becomes a small woody bush, it is harder to remove a sprig for cooking purposes. Also, there are fewer leaves than there are when the plant is young and green. Therefore, some people prefer to take a cutting of the old plant in the spring. By late summer, the cutting will have grown roots (if it has been first suspended in water for two or three weeks and then transplanted into a pot filled with potting soil, as is described in more detail for bay earlier in this chapter).

At that point, you can put the old plant into the compost heap and put the new one in its place. If you have a sunny window where you can keep the new, young plant in its pot through the winter, there will be a double benefit; the new plant will not have to survive the rigors in winter, and you will have fresh thyme all through the winter. The same method can be used with many of the other herbs, although it does mean a bit of work.

Let me review, then, the steps required for caring for the garden after it has been assembled. There may be weeds in chamomile if it is growing as a lawn, and a weed or two may grow out of the holes in the mulch at the base of other herbs. All the weeds should be removed if they interfere with the appearance of the garden or if they become large. Otherwise, there should be no weeding needed.

You may need to water occasionally, but you should not have to do so daily, except for potted bay or rosemary in very dry, sunny spells. In northern climates, you need to put down and take up a winter mulch once a year. Since the herbs are almost completely free of insects and diseases, you do not need to spray or dust. Every three years or so, you should divide some of the herbs. Care of the herb garden should take no more than two or three hours *a year* if you use a garden sprinkler to do the watering. I think that this is sufficiently easy to classify as "no work."

However, there is one last thing that I have omitted, but it hardly classifies as work, either.

THE HARVEST

For the most part, harvesting herbs in the summer consists of walking out to the garden with a pair of scissors and cutting off the amount you need at that moment. You may want to dry, freeze, or otherwise prepare some herbs for the winter. Freezing is generally the most suitable way to preserve leaves for the winter (short of bringing the plants indoors). One method of doing this is to put a teaspoonful of each herb in each section of an ice-cube tray, fill the tray with water, and then freeze. You can keep the different herbs in the freezer in plastic bags, labeled of course. Then, for soups, stews, or sauces, the cubes can simply be added near the end of cooking. The small amount of water won't matter, and the herbs will still have all of their flavor.

Some other specific suggestions are given in the catalog of the individual herbs. General and detailed directions for drying are given in the chapter on herbal teas. For all the herbs discussed in this chapter except Egyptian onions, the leaves are the parts you will use, so the part you want is always available all summer. You do not have to wait for something to get ripe the way you do with tomatoes; nor do you have to worry that it will pass its prime, as with zucchini. There are no dead flowers to remove, as you need to do to prolong blossoming in the flower garden. If you want to preserve herbs, you should know that it is generally believed that herbs are at their best in the early morning, before the sunlight has evaporated some of the oils that give the herbs their flavor. But that consideration is not very important for casual fresh use. In fact, for fresh use, the best time to cut a sprig or two is just before you reach that point in the cooking where you want to add the herbs, although a few minutes earlier than that does not make any significant difference. If you have to pick the herbs earlier, they will do better kept in damp paper towels.

For the most part, the flowers of the herbs are not used and are only in the way, although chive flowers are used sometimes. I like to see the flowers, so I generally harvest leaves from parts of the plant that are not blooming; but that is really not necessary. Also, sometimes I have to fight my way past bees to get to the herbs.

Therefore, I work on the part of the plant that is of least interest to the honey makers.

No garden can ever be completely free of labor, but after a perennial herb garden is properly set up, it is as close to that ideal as any type of garden can become.

Chapter 3
The Practical Annual Herbs

Most gardeners in the United States have experience with annual vegetables or flowers. Until recently, post-World War II flower gardens consisted largely of marigolds, petunias, zinnias, and other annuals or perennials treated as annuals. Only the rose remained of the truly popular perennials—and many gardeners found that roses were too much work to grow properly. While you might admire the clump of iris in your grandmother's garden or stoop to smell her lilies of the valley, these pleasures were definitely considered old fashioned. Less ambitious vegetable gardens were likely to consist merely of tomatoes, which are perennial plants raised as annuals. More ambitious gardens encompassed various other annuals, biennials, and perennials raised as annuals, such as lettuce, carrots, and peppers. Only the most serious gardeners raised their own asparagus or rhubarb as true perennials—and the first took a lot of work, while the second was hardly a staple.

Consequently, I assume that many of the readers of this book are likely to have had experience with growing annuals. For many people, however, the experience has been limited and often unsuccessful. This chapter details the ways to grow successfully herbs that are either annuals, biennials, or treated as annuals.

Since I have used that phrase, "annuals, biennials, or treated as annuals," it is worth while to make clear exactly what the distinctions are. True *annuals* are plants that grow from seed each year, flower, set seed, and die during the spring, summer, or fall. Common examples from the vegetable garden are lettuce and spinach. With such plants, the trick is to prevent them from flowering as long as possible. When these plants start to send up a stalk for flowers (flowers that later will become seeds)—this is called *bolting*—the plants have had it from the point of view of the gardener. Unless the seed is to be saved for another year, the best thing to do is to remove the plants to the compost heap and plant something else in their place.

True *biennials* winter over for a season, then flower, go to seed, and die. The most common types are those that store their food for wintering over in a fleshy root, for example the carrot and the beet, although cabbages are also biennials. Most biennials are harvested in their first year, so, from a gardener's point of view, they are annuals. Sometimes growing conditions will cause a biennial to flower in the first year instead of the second, causing the loss of the plant for food purposes. A biennial herb that is grown for its seed, however, cannot be used until the second year. As it happens, only one of the common herbs is actually treated as a biennial, although many really are biennials.

Many plants that are true *perennials* are grown as annuals. If a perennial such as the common bell pepper is carefully dug up in the fall and given good growing conditions indoors or in a greenhouse, it will continue to flower and fruit (at a somewhat slower pace than before) all winter; after its sojourn indoors, the pepper can be returned to the garden after all danger of frost, where it will thrive for another year. Then the performance can be repeated, provided the pepper has not grown too large for this sort of treatment. It is not the custom, however, to treat the pepper as a perennial in the northern United States, so most plants die when the first hard frost arrives. Many of the tropical plants that are grown in the north are actually, like the pepper, perennials treated as annuals.

This classification scheme is considerably confused, however, because it is not always clear whether a particular plant, given good treatment, is going to behave as an annual, biennial, or perennial. In some ways a clever classification scheme would be to label any plant that flowers in the first growing season as an annual, and any that flowers in the second season as a biennial, and any that takes longer than two years to flower as a perennial—but this is not the way the system works.

Growing conditions and time of planting can also have some effect on the plant's life span. For example, it is possible to plant some hardy annuals, such as spinach, in the fall. If spinach is protected from the worst of the winter, the plants will survive and behave as biennials. Different varieties of the same species can also be bred to be annuals, biennials, or perennials as well. Therefore, while it is often helpful to know the main tendency of a species, you should experiment from time to time to be sure exactly what you are dealing with.

In this chapter, I use the following rule of thumb: an annual is any herb that is cultivated starting from scratch each time. Thus, this classification will include some biennials, including some that must be grown for two years to obtain the seeds that you want to harvest. The following herbs are the ones that are treated individually in the catalog section of the book and that are annuals according to that test:

☐ **Basil** (a true annual).
☐ **Caraway** (a true biennial grown for its seeds).
☐ **Chervil** (a true annual).
☐ **Coriander** (a true annual).
☐ **Cumin** (a natural annual).
☐ **Dill** (a true annual).
☐ **Fennel** (a true perennial grown as an annual).
☐ **Garlic** (a true perennial grown as an annual).
☐ **Marjoram** (highly variable, but grown as an annual).
☐ **Nasturtium** (a true annual).
☐ **Parsley** (a true biennial, grown usually as an annual).

Having gone quite far in saying that these herbs all need to be started each year, I will now pull back a bit and say that it is often possible to grow many of the annuals without starting from scratch each year. But that is another story and will be saved for later.

The 11 annuals that are treated in the catalog section are not all of the possible herbs that one might grow. I have not given separate treatment to those annual herbs for which I prefer the perennial counterpart (German chamomile and summer savory) or to those that are little used in practical herb gardening.

The following plants, however, are all annuals—except that some are really biennials—for which the same general rules apply as to the others given more extensive space: angelica (a biennial), anise, borage, bugloss (a biennial grown for its flower's flavor), calendula, fenugreek, love-in-a-mist, mustard (for seed), mullein (a biennial), orache, perilla, safflower, sesame, and woad (a biennial). Of these, the ones most commonly used in cooking are angelica, anise, borage, calendula, fenugreek, mustard, perilla (in Japanese cooking), safflower, and sesame.

Angelica, anise, borage, and calendula have rather specialized purposes. Angelica is usually candied for use in cakes and English trifles, although it is also essential in making various cordials. Anise is used in candies and Indian cooking, including some curries; in European cooking anise flavor is commonly provided by a dash of Pernod or other anise-flavored liquor. Borage is used in cool drinks, mainly, although it can be added to yogurt or to salads. The petals of calendula are used for food coloring. Fenugreek and perilla are not common in European cooking. Mustard is very commonly used in bottled or dried form, but most people prefer to let others grow and prepare the seed. Safflower, like calendula, can be grown as a yellow food coloring (to replace saffron) but is better known for its oil. Unless you have a special press, the oil is inaccessible. Sesame simply takes too long to go to seed in most of the United States, as it has a long growing season.

THE SOIL

The main difference between perennials and annuals is, of course, that the soil has to be prepared every year for annuals (at best, every other year for caraway). Of course, you can prepare soil for annuals exactly as you would for perennials, but that is far too much work. Raised beds are neat (and essential in the case of poor drainage), but they are somewhat of a nuisance to dig up each year. Since annuals are likely to have smaller root systems than perennials, deep preparation of the soil with two layers of fertilization is also not needed. A permanent, or even a long-lasting, mulch just gets in the way of your digging—although an organic mulch can be dug into the soil to its lasting benefit. You would not want, however, to dig in an expensive organic mulch, such as cocoa beans or buckwheat hulls, every year. Finally, since the herbs will not be occupying the soil all year, you need to consider what should be done to protect your valuable resource—the soil—during the off-season.

The site for the annual herbs can be either in the same garden as the perennials, in a separate garden, in part of a vegetable garden, or in part of a flower garden. The one essential requirement for all annuals is that you must be able to spade the site as needed. Therefore, the annuals must be somewhat separated physically from the perennials or else you will disturb the permanent residents. This applies to annual herbs in a flower or vegetable garden as well as in a herb garden. While most of the annual herbs are not very showy, and therefore have limited use in a flower garden, nasturtiums are more often grown as flowers than as herbs. A dwarf form of dark purple basil can also be used to advantage as a border or backdrop among the flowers.

After considerable experimentation, however, I find that I prefer to grow the annual herbs, with the exception of basil and garlic, in a separate part of the herb garden. Basil sometimes winds up both in the herb garden and in the vegetable garden, because I like to grow a lot of basil. Garlic, which also gets a lot of use in our household, always is put in the vegetable garden, mainly because the amount I grow would take up too much space among the herbs.

Sunlight and good drainage are important for the annuals as well as for the perennials. If there is one spot in a bed of annual herbs that gets somewhat less than full sunlight, it can be reserved for parsley, which does well in either full sunlight or light shade. Fennel, dill, chervil, and coriander can also be grown in light shade. Fennel, dill, and coriander may not produce much seed in those situations—a distinct drawback if it is the seed you are after.

The same siting advice with regard to sunshine, therefore, applies to annuals as it does to perennials.

Amendments to the soil can also be, for the most part, the same as for the top layer of the perennial garden. On the other hand, some of the annuals are not from the sunny shores of the Mediterranean, which is where most of the perennials hail from. Plants whose ancestors grew in the open fields of northern Europe or in Caucasian meadows may be unhappy with soil that is too "sweet"—that is, alkaline. Where there is a lot of rain during most of the year, the soil gradually becomes more acid.

The plants that like soil on the acid side include basil, caraway, chervil, dill, garlic, and parsley. None of these are really acid-cravers (like blueberries or rhododendrons), but it is well to go easy on the wood ashes with the annual herbs and have a heavy hand with the compost. Cumin and marjoram are more Mediterranean in their habits, but neither demands a really sweet soil.

Nasturtium is famous for thriving in poor soil. While there are many stories about herbs that do better in poor soil than in good, the only one that seems to have any truth in it is the one about the nasturtium—and that relates principally to the blossoms. A nasturtium plant that gets a lot of nitrogen in the soil will produce lots of leaves, but few flowers (to some degree this is true of most plants, but even more so of nasturtium). I attribute this characteristic to the Peruvian homeland of the nasturtium, for the nasturtium is certainly a tropical plant. (Although it is always identified as a "tender annual," meaning quite susceptible to frost, I suspect that, like many tropical plants, the nasturtium is actually a perennial in its homeland.)

Where growing conditions do not change much during the year, evolution would dictate that as long as the conditions are excellent, there is not much need in wasting a lot of energy in producing flowers. When a particular site is exhausted of a major nutrient, however, multiple flowering is the best way to preserve the plant. In any case, tropical soils are notoriously deficient in nitrogen or other soluble nutrients. Only the steady rain of compostable material from the forest canopy keeps the soil fertile enough to support the forest. If the forest is cut, the soil soon becomes inhospitable to plants. This is the principal problem with tropical agriculture.

All of these conditions contribute to the nasturtium's deserved reputation as a plant to grow in poor soil. Consequently, it is probably a good idea to hold off on the compost and certainly go easy on such high-nitrogen amendments as cottonseed meal where nasturtiums are concerned.

Since the soil must be prepared every year for annuals, you normally have to dig it every spring. (I say "normally," since there are some possible exceptions dealt with later in the chapter.) If the soil has been mulched or if there is other organic matter in the top layer of the soil (that is, a cover crop, also discussed later in the chapter), it should be dug in at this time. I do this before adding any amendments except for compost. I use the same method of digging as for the perennial garden; that is, I dig a trench, save the soil, and then dig along one face of the trench so that the trench "moves" through the garden, leaving a heap of turned-over soil behind it. Then the saved soil is used to fill up the trench at the other end of the plot.

Other amendments can then be added. Nevertheless, most annual herbs do not require as great a quantity of nutrients in the soil as perennials do, simply because some nutrients are being added each year. Plants that are being grown for their leaves do better with high-nitrogen amendments such as cottonseed meal or blood meal. Both are fairly expensive, however, and not absolutely necessary if you have used a lot of compost. Dried manure, which is available from garden stores, is less expensive and—although it is not very high in nutrients—is probably sufficient in most soils. Wood ashes can be used sparingly. Rock powders, such as rock phosphate or greensand, are excellent amendments for the long run, although they may not make much difference at first. All these amendments can be added before hoeing and raking. The hoeing and raking process will get them deep enough in the soil for planting, and then their nutrients will trickle down as the plants grow. This is a more realistic form of trickle-down economics than is usually practiced by the government.

If you stick to organic amendments, as listed above, you should continue to add them every year. There is little chance that you will ever get too much in the soil. An exception can be made for lime—which, in any case, is probably too alkaline for many annual herbs. If you use lime, you should only do so once every three or four years.

Compost and organic mulches, in particular, should be added each year. Sun and rain gradually break down compost, producing a lifeless soil. It is this combination of sunlight and rain, remember, that wrecks soil in the tropics if the tree cover is removed.

PLANTING

For the most part, annual herbs are planted as seeds in the ground. This is quite different from the perennials, none of which are planted directly in the garden in most climates. Since I expect that you are more likely to have planted annual flowers or vegetables in the past, I assume that you have a general idea about how seeds are planted. Nevertheless, there are some helpful hints that you may not know and some practices that you may never have tried.

A major difference between the perennials and the annuals is in the number of plants that you will need. While it is possible to get by with a single plant of nearly all the perennials (except, for instance, chives), you will need rows or plots of most annuals to get enough for a family to use. The needs actually range from about a half-dozen plants of basil (although I plant more) or dill to perhaps as many as a hundred garlic plants if you use garlic extensively. In all cases, you need to modulate the number of plants to the actual use patterns in your family. In general, you should try to err on the side of planting too many seeds—in the beginning especially, when you are less sure of what your needs will be.

Timing

Most herbs that are true annuals need to be planted in the later part of the spring, since they are the ones that are most likely to be tender. Similarly, most herbs that are true biennials or perennials can be planted earlier in the spring, sometimes as soon as the soil is dry enough and warm enough to be dug without causing it to compact from the spade. While this is a handy rule of thumb for plants in general, the particular herbs discussed in this book present a wide spectrum of complications. For example, members of the carrot family—such as parsley, fennel, and dill—tend to like an early start, even though parsley is a biennial, fennel is a perennial raised as an annual, and dill is a true annual. Here is a rough order of planting.

Late Fall. In my climate, I always plant garlic in November. It emerges in the spring earlier than I would want to disturb the ground. I am told that caraway can also be planted in the fall, but I suspect that such a planting would be much earlier in the fall, aiming to get the caraway to go to seed the following year instead of following its natural biennial bent.

Late Winter. Cumin needs a long growing season; it is best to start it indoors. If you are going to start your own basil from seed, instead of buying flats as I often do, you can also start basil at this time.

Very Early Spring. Parsley can be planted as soon as the ground can be worked—and since it is a slow-germinating and slow-growing plant, this is the time to do it. Later plantings will do all right, but you will not have parsley until later as well. If you are not trying to get a year's jump on caraway, it can also be planted early.

Early to Middle Spring. Plant chervil, dill, and fennel. Dill may need to be replanted two or three times, at two- or three-week intervals, to have a sufficient supply all summer.

Late Spring. When temperatures reach at least 45°F every day, you can plant marjoram and coriander. Another rule of thumb that goes back to the old days may not be suitable for suburban or urban gardeners. It was suggested that the farmer should remove his trousers and sit on the bare soil. If the farmer was comfortable, so would the seeds be. If you have grown cumin and basil from seed, or can obtain plants, they can be set out now. For a good supply of both coriander leaves and seeds, you will need to replant coriander every two or three weeks until early summer.

Seed Depth

The seed packet will give you advice on the proper depth for each kind of seed, but there is a good rule of thumb that most gardeners use, not only for herbs but for all annuals. Seeds should be planted at about the same depth as the size of the seed itself.

Since most herb seeds are fairly small (certainly as compared to pumpkin seeds, for instance), for most of the herbs this means virtually scattering the seeds on top of the ground. Garlic, on the other hand, is not planted from seeds, but from individual cloves. The same rule of thumb applies, however; the cloves should be planted so there is about as much soil above them as the length of the clove itself—usually about an inch.

The best way to handle small, but not tiny, seeds is to plant them on top of the ground and then sprinkle sifted compost over them. Compost can be sifted nicely by putting a piece of machine cloth (a kind of coarse wire mesh, with holes roughly ¼ inch on a side) over a bucket. Pick up a handful of compost and rub it onto the top of the machine cloth. Sifted compost will fall into the bucket, while stones and small twigs will stay on top. The material in the bucket can then easily be spread by lightly tossing a handful at a time over the seeds from a height of 3 or 4 feet. You do not want clumps of compost, but a fairly uniform layer that is about ⅛ inch deep on top the seeds. If you cover the seeds enough so that they cannot be seen by birds, you probably have gone far enough.

Very small seeds, such as parsley, need no covering at all. It is, however, a good idea to mix the seeds with sifted compost, dried manure, or fine sand before sowing them. This mixture keeps the seed farther apart. Otherwise, too many plants will grow in one place. Even with the other material mixed in, too many plants will tend to grow in one place. Thinning is discussed shortly.

Garlic can be planted at a fairly uniform depth by making a row of holes with the handle of a hoe or rake. One clove goes in each hole, pointy side up. (In really good soil, you do not need to make the holes at all. You can press the cloves to the required depth with your fingers.) After each clove is planted, it is a simple matter to collapse the hole around the garlic. It is important to make sure that the hole is really collapsed so that the soil touches the garlic on all sides.

Rows Versus Plots

Most people still plant vegetables in rows, so that you can more easily cultivate between the vegetables. When a gardener says *cultivate*, he or she is referring to the process of removing weeds, usually by digging up the top layer of the soil with a hoe or with a machine. Pulling weeds by hand is also cultivating, but for some reason, most gardeners call that activity *pulling weeds* or *weeding*. In either case, the main purpose is the same—to remove the weeds. Stirring up the top layer of the soil may also have some benefits in areas where the soil is likely to crust over.

Herbs are often planted in rows, especially if they are grown in the vegetable garden. Rows are probably essential for farming, and possibly essential for large family gardens. The only way that you can mechanically cultivate a garden is if it has been planted in rows. For the herb garden, however—unless you are growing herbs commercially—it is unlikely that enough herbs will be planted to make the use of mechanical cultivators necessary. Most herb gardeners—and many vegetable gardeners—have abandoned rows in favor of plots.

In a garden plot, plants are spaced approximately equal distances apart in each direction. In rows, the space between the rows is often four or five times the space between the plants, especially if mechanical cultivation is used. It should be clear that you can grow more plants per square foot in plots than you can in rows. For vegetable gardeners, growing more plants is one of the principal benefits of using plots instead of rows. Even for annual herbs, however, the number of plants needed is relatively small. Space considerations are not so essential. For herbs, the other advantage of growing plants in plots is more useful. This is that the herbs are close enough together to shade out the weeds, making weeding less of a chore.

On the other hand, it is generally somewhat easier to mulch rows than plots. There is a lot more hand work with a plot in getting the mulch around each plant. Mulched rows and plots do not need cultivation in any case. The mulch prevents the weeds from getting started (and makes any that do manage to break through easy to remove). So if you mulch, there are arguments on both sides of the plot-row question.

I grow all my annual herbs (and most of my vegetables) in plots instead of in rows. About the only time I vary this is when I grow a row of herbs as an edging (say, garlic, nasturtium, or dwarf basil). Since space is only a minor concern for the herbs, I think that the main reason for this is that I like the looks of plots better than the looks of rows. Mulching the plots is enough work that I often do not mulch the thicker growths, such as dill and fennel, saving my mulch for plants that grow farther apart, such as basil, or plants that do not provide much cover to shade out weeds, such as garlic. If you have a good, thick stand of the herb, skipping the mulching does not do too much harm, although you will have more weeds than if you mulched.

Germination

Generally, it takes from one to four weeks for seeds to germinate, although there are various exceptions. Plants in the parsley family can be very slow to germinate and may take over a year for some individual seeds. With parsley itself, I generally try some trick to speed germination. The trick that has worked best for me has been to plant the seeds and then water them with boiling water. It sounds as if it would be dangerous for the seeds, but I have always gotten good results using a kettle of water that was actually boiling when it left the stove.

Of course, the parsley is watered with regular, hose-temperature water after the first day. The boiling water is just to get the seeds' attention.

All seeds should be given water of some temperature when they are first planted. The seeds need to be told that they are in a suitable environment, and the best way to send them a message is to get them wet. Unless the weather is very rainy, I usually water every day until the seedlings have emerged and appear to be strong enough to go a few days on their own. Certainly, the ground should be kept fairly moist until after the true leaves have appeared. (For most plants, the first set of leaves does not resemble the plants of the adult. This is particularly true of *dicots*, which have two "seed leaves." *Monocots*, such as garlic or other members of the lily family, have only one seed leaf, which is rather like a blade of grass.)

Thinning

When seeds are planted directly in the ground, it is almost always necessary to thin. The only herb planted directly in the ground that I do not thin is garlic. Garlic comes up reliably enough that it can be safely planted the right distance apart to begin with, roughly 3 or 4 inches. If there are a few gaps where the garlic failed to appear, it is not a major tragedy.

Plants started inside, such as basil or cumin, are thinned in their containers before they are set out into the garden. In fact, if they are planted far enough apart in their first seed bed, each plant that emerges can be put into an individual pot. In that case, they are not really thinned at all, but the effect is the same.

Thinning is, of course, removing excess plants. If two plants are growing from exactly the same spot in the garden, neither one will do very well since they are in competition for light and for soil nutrients. Plants are removed from the row or plot when they are a couple of inches high, either by pulling the tiny plants out or by clipping them at ground level with scissors. Pulling them out sometimes has the unwanted result of removing a plant that you were intending to leave, since one plant can be lifted by the roots of its close neighbor, but in my opinion, taking plants out with scissors is harder work. That means that I generally pull the plants out by the roots.

Rows are easier to thin than plots. Most seed packets will have the appropriate distance for the initial planting and for the thinning written on the back of the packet. If you use a plot instead of a row, the distance between plants should be the same in all directions as the "thin to" directions on the seed packet. Unmulched plants should be slightly closer than mulched ones, however. The adult plants should touch or almost touch if you are not going to mulch. If you mulch, the plants can be any distance apart that is farther than the touching distance of adult plants. The greater the distance, the easier the mulch is to handle, but the garden will require more space and more mulch, so you'll want to compromise.

If you plant in plots or rows, smaller seeds will require less thinning if they are mixed with sifted compost, dried manure, or sand, as noted earlier. With plots, you can simply scatter the seed-compost mixture over the plot. If you do a good job of both mixing and seeding, the amount of thinning will be much less. In rows, you sow the seed-compost mixture along the row with the same beneficial result. I prefer to use compost or manure for this maneuver, since this last little bit of organic matter contributes to a good start for the seedlings.

Some gardeners have reservations about thinning. After all, having paid for the seeds, they don't want to throw away or cut down plants. Thinning is necessary, however, unless you devote hours to getting all the seeds exactly where you want them and unless the seeds all germinate. Unfortunately, many herbs—especially parsley—are notorious for poor germination. It is better to plant somewhat more thickly than you need, and then thin.

About the only alternative to thinning is to transplant some of the too-closely spaced plants. Again, this is not suitable for many annual herbs; they do not transplant well. About the only herb that it would make sense to transplant instead of thinning would be marjoram. Many of the annual herbs, such as parsley, dill, and fennel, have long single roots called *taproots*. (Remember that these herbs are related to carrots.) The taproots break when you try to transplant the herbs. Although transplanting herbs that have long tap-roots is possible, it often fails.

Seeds are still inexpensive. Best results are obtained by planting more seeds than you will need, then thinning. It is not really wasteful when the only other alternative is to grow small, weak plants.

WHERE TO PLANT

For the most part, annual herbs are not so attractive as most of the perennial herbs, although some, such as nasturtium, are grown mainly for their looks by many gardeners. Aside from nasturtium, none of the main herbs covered in this book have flowers that are showy at all. Caraway, chervil, cumin, dill, fennel, and parsley are all members of the carrot family (to one degree or another—like most large families it is hard to sort out all the relationships). This means that they have a type of flower that is called an *umbel* (from *umbrella*, since it looks a little like an umbrella) and very small leaves. The common weed Queen Anne's Lace (really a wild carrot) is typical of this family, and has a well-defined umbel. Since an umbel consists of many tiny flowers, it is not especially attractive. Marjoram and basil both have flower spikes, along the lines of a delphinium or saliva, but much smaller and less showy. Garlic looks like an onion plant, and cannot be counted upon to bloom reliably. Therefore, there is a limited use of annual herbs in flower gardens. Aside from nasturtium, the most common ornamental use is the occasional planting of a small, dark purple variety of basil, mainly for the color of its leaves.

Some people put herbs in their vegetable gardens because they believe in companion planting. Companion planting is the practice of growing two plants together on the assumption that one or both of the plants will benefit thereby. Since herbs are little bothered by insect pests, although not completely free of them, the assumption is that something about the herb must repel the insects. Therefore, planting herbs among the vegetables is a good idea, because the herbs will keep insects away from the vegetables.

Garlic, with its strong odor, is particularly favored by com-panion planters. Regrettably, the few scientific studies of this idea suggest that it does no good at all. Also, lists that you see of companion plants often contradict other lists of companion plants. It is difficult to see that there could be any scientific truth involved. Just for your information, however, here is a typical list of herbs beneficial to your other plants:

- [ ] Anise seeds make coriander germinate faster.
- [ ] Basil will not grow near rue, nor vice versa.
- [ ] Bee balm improves the flavor of tomatoes.
- [ ] Caraway will not grow near peas or fennel.
- [ ] Chives improve the flavor and growth of carrots.
- [ ] Coriander hinders seed formation in fennel.
- [ ] Dill likes cabbage, hates carrots.
- [ ] Fennel is disliked by most plants.
- [ ] Garlic protects roses.
- [ ] German chamomile promotes growth of cabbage.
- [ ] Horseradish makes potatoes healthy.
- [ ] Hyssop improves the yield of grapevines.
- [ ] Lovage planted here and there helps most plants.
- [ ] Mint helps both cabbages and tomatoes.
- [ ] Nasturtiums keep away squash bugs.
- [ ] Oregano repels cabbage butterflies from broccoli.
- [ ] Parsley mixed with carrot seed repels carrot flies.
- [ ] Pennyroyal repels cabbage maggots.
- [ ] Sage and rosemary help each other.
- [ ] Thyme makes other herbs more fragrant.

I did not make these notions up! Many people believe them, although I cannot see any way that a garden could be planned around these ideas. Perhaps you would start out with a mixed stand of cabbages and German chamomile, surrounded by carrots mixed with chives, pennyroyal, and parsley. Somehow you have to keep the mint and the tomatoes close to the cabbages, though. If you are not worried about the shade that lovage will produce, you should put a 5-foot-tall lovage in the middle of each patch. The rue and the basil will be at opposite ends of the garden, while the fennel will be off somewhere in a plot by itself. It is not enough that scientific tests of these ideas have shown they do not work; the ideas themselves are impossible to execute consistently.

There is a good reason to put annual herbs in the vegetable garden, however. Most vegetables are annuals, biennials, or perennials treated as annuals—in other words, most vegetables are similar in their habits to the "annual" herbs I have been discussing. Therefore, the garden is dug each year and fresh seed or new plants are put into the soil for both annual herbs and most vegetables. Probably the most practical place for the annual herbs is among the annual vegetables. They need not take up much space in the garden. If you plant in rows, a couple of rows of herbs, rows the size you generally use for a single vegetable, would be sufficient herbs for most families. If you need more of a particular herb, it can be planted elsewhere. Basil and garlic are two herbs that can be used in more abundance than most. The basil could be set out among the tomatoes. The garlic could be planted in a separate row on its own (in addition to the two rows previously mentioned), or perhaps used as a border along the side of the garden.

If you garden in plots instead of rows, a plot 4 feet by 8 feet would almost do. If you grew all the annual herbs I have been discussing, you probably would need at least half of another plot that size as well.

As with all plants, the size of the adult plant will have some effect on how the garden should be laid out. All of the herbs discussed here are on the tall, thin side except for basil, chervil, parsley, and nasturtium. Despite the skinniness of some of the herbs, they can still shade each other; the different heights should be taken into account when planning. Roughly, fennel is the tallest of the skinny plants, cumin the shortest, with dill, coriander, and marjoram somewhere in between. Parsley is short in its first year, especially the curly leaved French type, although it grows quite tall if you let it go to seed during a second year. Chervil is slightly taller than first-year parsley.

While most herbs do not come in varieties, the few that do are available in various sizes. Basil can be quite large, almost as large as a bell pepper plant. That version is often called "lettuce leaf" basil. There are both green and purple varieties of dwarf basil, each of which is only about half as tall as the lettuce-leaf variety. (Sometimes, also, various species related to basil are identified as basil. These relatives have different habits and different flavors from true basil.) Nasturtium has even a greater variation than basil within the same species, since it can be grown either as a vine or as a small "bush," like green beans. For the herb garden, I generally grow the bush-type nasturtium, although there is nothing wrong with the vine type.

While on the subject of the varieties of nasturtium, let me digress to remark on double and single blossoms. Since nasturtium is grown most of the time as a flower instead of a herb, plant breeders have developed varieties with bigger and, they believe, better blossoms. Most of the nasturtium seeds available in catalogs are for double-blossomed varieties because the flowers are showier. I have never tried the double-blossomed type, however, since I suspect that breeders who are worrying about bigger and more complex blossoms may not take into account the needs of someone who likes a few nasturtium leaves in a summer salad or an inexpensive substitute for capers. Also, double-blossomed nasturtiums (or hollyhocks or any old, traditional flower that has been bred in new forms) do not look right to me. If God had intended nasturtiums to have double blossoms . . .

While herbs are less subject to diseases than other plants, it is a good idea to follow the common practice of rotating the crop; that is, planting different herbs in the same spot in succeeding years. Not only can some diseases or pests that are injurious to a particular herb linger in the soil, but also different plants have different nutritional requirements. If the same herb is planted in the same spot year after year, there may be some single element that is consistently removed from the soil. Rotation prevents this. Actually, you need to do more than just to vary the specific plants; you need to rotate with the plant families in mind. All the members of the carrot family, for instance, have similar nutritional needs and susceptibilites. Rotating between dill and fennel will not make much difference. Instead you should look for plants from an entirely different family, such as basil or garlic.

MAKING ANNUAL HERBS MORE PRACTICAL

Buying seed and digging every year may not be your idea of a good way to spend your time or your money. Be of good cheer; there is hope for a better way, although I grant you that this better way is not perfect.

Most annual herbs as defined here go to seed in their first year. In the wild, these seeds fall to the ground, and, with no care from human gardeners, new plants spring up that year or the following one. There is no reason why the same cannot happen in your own herb garden. The seeds are free and no digging is required.

The hitch is that not all seeds that land in the soil spring up to become new plants, in the wild or in the garden. Sometimes seeds fail to germinate, or they are eaten by birds or other creatures, or they land in an unfortunate place. For the annual herbs, however, some are quite good about producing offspring. These offspring are called *volunteers*. While you cannot count on volunteers to fill your garden every year with all the annual herbs, you can count on some of them to produce volunteers in most years.

Probably the best-known herb for self-seeding (producing volunteers) is dill. Dill reaches the seed stage very quickly. If all the seeds are not harvested for use in pickles, the seeds fall to the ground in the vincinity of the original plants. Sometimes two or three crops of dill will be produced this way during a season if conditions are right. In fact, the stand of dill can become too thick for its own good if you never harvest any of the seeds. Most years, however, you can count on enough self-seeding to keep the crop going with little or no intervention from you except some weeding.

This brings us to other problems with self-seeding. For the method to work, the herbs almost have to be grown in plots instead of rows. Also, you cannot mulch. Since dill can be grown in a fairly thick stand—in fact, it almost has to be grown that way, or a brisk wind will blow the plants down—these problems are not major for dill. If the stand of dill is thick enough to shade out all the weeds, however, it may also be too dense to permit young dill plants to get started. The next year, though, the seeds should grow, after their parents have succumbed to frost. In that way, the plot can be carried from year to year.

Gardeners commonly count on dill to produce volunteers, but the self-seeding method works as well with the other true annuals that are sufficiently hardy. These include chervil, coriander, and marjoram. It is somewhat less successful with perennials grown as annuals, perhaps because they have no need to start new plants each year in their native regions. Another problem with using self-seeding is that this method is not compatible with crop rotation. I find that after a few seasons, self-seeding a particular patch begins to be nonproductive, so I start again in another place and plant the area where the volunteers were with a herb from a different family.

Plants that are not especially hardy, such as basil, cumin, and nasturtium cannot self-seed in temperate climates. You have no choice but to plant every year. In fact, basil and cumin should be started inside—although you can usually buy started basil from local garden stores. Nasturtium grows fast enough to plant directly in the ground in the late spring.

The biennials are a separate matter. Parsley is grown for its leaves, so most people prefer to treat it as an annual. If it is given a little protection, it will survive to go to seed. By the time it does, however, it is too late to count on any of the seeds germinating in time for a new crop that year. Therefore, if you hope to maintain a population of parsley, you have to maintain two populations, one for harvesting, and the other for seeding. Parsley is one of the few herbs that have been bred in different varieties. Watch out for hybrid parsley if you are interested in reseeding, since it will not breed true (and may not breed at all).

The other biennial on the short list of practical herbs is caraway. Caraway has a habit much like parsley, but it is grown primar ily for its seed instead of its leaves. Therefore, if you want caraway to reseed, you must refrain from harvesting a few of the seed heads. You must also maintain two populations, as with parsley.

Garlic is a totally separate matter. I have never heard of anyone growing garlic from seed, although I am sure that it must be possible. There is no practical hope for growing garlic without planting each year. In fact, if you leave garlic in the ground (I sometimes do as a result of a harvesting error), you get a clump of skinny plants. This condition is caused by a number of garlic bulbs growing close together and crowding each other. If you dig these small bulbs up and replant them several inches apart, you can get better bulbs, but not as good as the ones produced by planting cloves the winter before. If you try to replant bulbs from last year's unharvested garlic, you should keep the ground around the trans- planted bulbs very moist, as they tend to wither from the disruption to their root system.

CARING FOR THE ANNUALS

The biggest difference between annuals and perennials, aside from planting time, is that true annuals or plants grown as annuals are not there in the winter. Except for biennials that are being carried through the winter, there is no need to protect the plants with mulch. This does not mean that you should not mulch in the winter, however. Something else that *is* there in the winter re- quires protection: the soil.

A lot can happen to the soil in the winter and most of what happens is bad. Winter rains and melting snow leach out the nu- trients. Freezing and thawing breaks up the crumb of the soil. Dried soil can be blown away by winter winds. On a warm and sunny winter day the sun burns the organic material in the top layer of the soil. Unprotected, the soil simply loses too much of the good things that you worked into it in the previous spring, so you are starting all over again.

There are two essentially different approaches to winter soil protection for the annual garden. The first one is simply to mulch the annual garden much as you do during the summer. An organic mulch is preferred because it can be dug into the soil in the spring when you are digging the garden for planting. The mulch does not need to be removed—although if you use a lot of straw or hay as a mulch, you may find that it interferes with your digging and that its decay robs the soil somewhat of nitrogen. Sawdust, which is a suitable winter mulch in other regards, takes even more nitrogen and does so for a longer time. In fact, if you mulch with anything other than compost, it will tend to remove nitrogen, so you should be liberal with a high-nitrogen fertilizer, such as cottonseed or blood meal, when you dig the mulch into the soil in the spring. Compost, however, is an ideal mulch for the winter garden, although it does lose a little of its power over the winter. Fresh compost should be added as you dig the garden as well. The real problem with compost, however, is that almost no one has enough compost to use as a mulch over all of a moderate-size garden.

I use chopped leaves. When leaves have been chopped—which can be done with a shredder attachment on a lawn mower, or by running over them with a rotary lawn mower, or by a shredder—they do not blow away. Furthermore, this practice gets rid of the leaves in the fall, and chopped leaves are easy to dig into the soil, unlike straw or hay. The leaves become most available just at the time you should be looking for something to cover the bare soil in the garden.

A layer of chopped leaves about an inch thick does an excellent job of protecting the soil. When the spring arrives, the bottom of the layer is beginning to compost itself, although not very thoroughly. In a few days after the ground has been dug, the leaves decay completely. Although they may be robbing a little nitrogen as they decay, the speed at which they go means that you do not need to worry about continued nitrogen loss.

Researchers have found that digging leaves into the soil tends to reduce productivity during the first year, but increases productivity in succeeding years. Using chopped leaves every year does not seem to me to interfere with productivity, although I have not carried out controlled experiments. My soil has improved noticeably since I started digging the leaves into it.

A thinner layer of chopped leaves can even be used where you are not going to dig in the spring. If you planted garlic in the fall, it will thrust right through a ½-inch layer of chopped leaves in the early spring. Most plants that start from seed will not have the power that garlic has to penetrate the mulch, therefore the garlic bed will remain weed-free until you are ready to harvest the garlic.

I am doubtful about using chopped leaves on a bed that I expect to self-seed, however, so I abandon the dill patch to the elements to see what volunteers I will get.

The other approach to winter care of the soil in an annual garden is to use what is either called *green manure* or a *cover crop*. A cover crop is grown after the herbs have been removed or killed by frost. The cover crop needs to get started before the frost is too heavy, so a good practice is to sow the seed in late August or early September. The cover crop will start the germination process even before the herbs are gone, but by the time the cover crop is large enough to present any possible competition for the herbs, winter will have arrived and the herbs will be no more.

For a good cover crop, you need to plant something that will grow very fast and is sufficiently hardy to withstand a certain amount of frost. With these requirements in mind, the ideal cover crop for a herb garden is rye.

You probably associate rye bread with northern Europe— Germany, Scandinavia, and Russia. This is the right association, because rye can be grown successfully much farther north than wheat can, which is why rye became a staple in the North. In fact, rye was probably introduced to cultivation as a weed in wheat fields, but farmers eventually noticed that the rye survived weather that wrecked the wheat harvest.

When you grow rye as a cover crop, however, the aim is not to obtain seeds for grinding into flour. You will dig in the crop before it sets seed. This accounts for the other name given to the practice— green manure. Like adding manure to soil, digging in the rye improves the soil. Not only does it create a better soil structure by adding organic matter, it also adds nutrients to the soil, especially nitrogen. Where did it get the nitrogen? Out of the soil, of course, But the secret is that the rye got the nitrogen and other beneficial elements from layers of the soil below the area where the roots of herbs penetrate. The rye also locks up the nutrients that would otherwise be leached into lower layers of the soil, releasing them again after it has been dug back into the soil.

Of course, some plants can get nitrogen from the air as well as from the soil. Such plants make even better cover crops than rye. All the plants that have this ability are legumes, of which the most familiar are peas and beans. Conceivably, you could use peas as a cover crop in a herb garden, since they grow fast and do not mind a bit of frost. I have never heard of anyone doing this, but some year I will try it. Farmers often use alfalfa, which is a legume, as a cover crop, but it does not grow fast enough for home gardeners to use. You really need to give up a field for at least half the year to make growing alfalfa worthwhile. The same applies to other legumes that are commonly grown as cover crops by farmers.

68

Buckwheat and rye grass are practical alternatives to rye for the herb garden. Neither offers much in the way of benefits that rye does not also offer, although buckwheat can be sown later than rye (for spring growth) and has deeper root penetration. Rye seed is available from major seed companies that cater to home gardeners, but you might have some trouble finding buckwheat seed except from a farm supplier.

In the spring, shortly before you are ready to plant, you simply dig the cover into the soil. In a small garden, you can hoe to break up the stems. In fact, especially if you have a rotary mower (the kind with a whirling blade), you might want to mow before you dig to reduce both the chores of hoeing and digging. Another alternative is to dig and chop the crop with a mechanical tiller. The idea is to get the seeds in the soil as soon as possible after the green manure is in place, so the young herbs will get the most benefit from the nutrients before these chemical necessities return to the depths of the subsoil.

The other benefit of the cover crop, of course, is the same benefit gained using a mulch. Because the crop is in place all during the winter, the soil is protected from the ravages of winter. Therefore, the cover crop needs to be sown quite thickly. Additionally, the thicker the cover crop is, the more green manure you will have in the spring.

Cover crops cannot be used, of course, in any place where you are not going to dig in the spring. Some people do put a cover crop around perennials, but they have to be careful in the spring not to disturb the roots of the permanent inhabitants. Overwintering biennials and herbs planted in the fall, volunteers, and garlic are not candidates for cover cropping at all. For them, you should stick to the mulch.

The annual herbs are sufficiently useful that no one should be without them. It is true that you can increasingly buy garlic, parsley, dill, and basil fresh in supermarkets or other food stores. In fact, if you know where to look and are near a large city, you can probably buy fresh coriander. No doubt someday chervil, fennel, and marjoram will all be available, and perhaps even nasturtium leaves (although watercress, which is often available, fills the same need as nasturtium leaves). Since this short list covers all the annuals that you need to have fresh (perfectly good seeds are available for caraway and cumin, for instance), the need for growing annuals is less great than the need for growing perennials.

Nevertheless, annuals are easy to grow (except for chervil in my garden) and your own will always be fresher than any you can buy. Furthermore, growing your own annual herbs is cheaper than buying them. If you have a little space and do not mind doing some digging each spring, you ought to include the annuals in your plan.

Chapter 4
The Practical Herb Teas

Herbal teas have become quite popular in the past dozen years or so. Brands that once were available only in health stores now appear in a section of their own on supermarket shelves. I presume that most people who buy these commercial herbal teas do so because either the purchasers do not want to drink something containing caffeine or because they do not really like the taste of coffee or tea. It is also possible that the buyer believes that there is some medicinal value to herbal teas.

People who buy herbal teas should read labels more carefully. Many of the popular brands of herbal teas contain real tea or other sources of caffeine, for example. If you drink these brands, you are not avoiding caffeine. Others contain various ingredients that few of us would think of as herbs, including tree leaves and various other natural products used as flavorings or colorings. This is not to say that there is anything wrong with commercial herbal teas, just that most of them are not what I would call herb teas.

(I will make a distinction between a *herbal* tea that may or may not contain actual herbs and a *herb* tea that is 100 percent composed of herbs and water. Sometimes herb teas are called *tisanes*, from a Greek word that, oddly enough, means "crushed barley." Despite the origin of the word, this is a perfectly good name for herb teas. It just sounds affected to me, perhaps because the accent is on the last syllable.)

One year when I was working in an office, I gave jars of one of my homemade herb teas to several of my coworkers who always drank herbal tea at our "coffee break." These herbal-tea drinkers were instant converts to the herb-tea idea. In fact, when I have run into one of them in later years, I am always asked if I still make that great herb tea.

Unfortunately, I don't know whether or not I still make the herb tea that wowed them in the office. I have never settled on a particular blend for herb tea but am constantly experimenting. (I have the same problem when I cook; I hate to make the same thing the same way twice.) There are certain constants. I always use a lot of lemon balm, for instance, since I can't seem to keep it from springing up all over the herb garden and since I like a lemony tea. If I have chamomile blossoms available, I use them. Chamomile really does seem to impart a soothing quality to tea. I always use some mint, but not too much, since I don't want a mentholated tea, just—as the old cigarette ad says—"a hint of mint."

After that, everything else is experimental. I often include sage. Lemon thyme is a part of the tea almost as often. I have tried oregano, rosemary, thyme, winter savory, marjoram, and even tarragon with pleasant—or perhaps unnoticeable—results. These all seem to blend fairly well with the basic lemon-chamomile-mint combination.

I used comfrey along with these combinations until I read that it may be harmful to the health. Dill, fennel, and caraway make interesting teas, alone or in combination with other herbs, but they do not seem to me to belong with the lemon and mint. Fennel, chamomile, tarragon, and chervil, or some combination that includes fennel with one or two of the others, makes an interesting licorice-flavored tea—not what I would want first thing in the morning, but all right for a break in the afternoon. This flavor can be improved by adding star anise, a Chinese herb. Caraway or cumin—leaves, not seeds—can also be used in combination with chamomile or other herbs to produce an interesting flavor. Dill tea is a wake-up idea that not everyone likes. (Dill seeds used to be chewed to keep awake before caffeine pills or amphetamines were invented.)

There are some herbs that would never do as a refreshing tea. Chives, Egyptian onions, lovage, and garlic might add a lot to a bouillon, but I would hardly call the result a tea. Neither bay nor parsley seems to belong in teas, although probably someone other than me has given that idea a try. Actually, bay tea is suggested in one of the popular herb books. Basil might contribute a lot to a tea if used fresh, but dried basil does not have much flavor. Coriander leaves by themselves have a taste that many people find unpleasant, which I suspect would carry over to the tea, although I have not performed that experiment.

A number of herbs that are not discussed in detail in this book can also be used in teas. These include anise, hyssop, angelica, woodruff, lemon verbena, horehound, German chamomile, fever-few, catnip, rose, rose geranium, perilla, costmary, lavender, mullein, and wintergreen. Some herbs, such as rue and tansy, may provoke allergic reactions or, in large quantities, be poisonous so the experimenter should check the herb in several references if it is not described here.

A few herbs, such as bee balm (monarda), need to be boiled to produce tea. Boiled bee balm leaves makes a very nice tea, by the way. This use accounts for its common name of a few centuries ago, Oswego tea. I have read that drinking Oswego tea was one of the ways that the Colonists protested George III's tea tax. Actually, it is better than a protest drink, although it is not the same thing as real tea, either.

TEAS AS MEDICINE

Many of the herbs were originally valued as medicines, long before they had any other known use. Cuneiform tablets from ancient Sumeria, five thousand years old, tell of medicinal uses for cumin and thyme. Herbals—books that primarily described the effects on the body various plants were supposed to have—were a thriving cottage industry in the early days of book publishing. Even today, most herb books devote at least some space to these ancient remedies. I have distinctly mixed feelings on that subject, however.

On the one hand, I do not think that it would be advisable to treat an illness of any severity with herb teas. The conflicting and confusing claims made by the ancient and modern herbalists are mostly unverified. Furthermore, herbs grown in different gardens vary considerably in any effects they do have. If a herb contains an important medicine, such as digitalis in foxglove or aspirin in willow bark, you are much safer getting a prescription for digitalis from your doctor or buying aspirin at the drugstore than you are going to the garden or forest for your cure. Furthermore, the herbs that do contain powerful chemicals that help a particular condition gener-ally contain other powerful chemicals as well. Medicines may have been improved from the essential elements found in a particular herb. The aspirin precursor in willow bark is even harder on the stomach than the artificial aspirin in a bottle is; aspirin was invented with the idea of keeping the pain-killing qualities while getting rid of the irritant.

On the other hand, given the example of the many medicines that are derived directly from plants, it is hard to think that the herbs—which were used for medicinal purposes long before they made their way into the kitchen—have no effect on the body. Therefore, I feel that you should know what medicinal effects are supposed to be in any teas you make. As noted, herbs from different gardens will vary; do not expect that every tea will work as described.

Relaxing or Soothing. Chamomile, mint, lemon balm, woodruff, bay, lavender, valerian, and, it is sometimes said, dill.

Digestive. Cumin, coriander, caraway, fennel, marjoram, savory, lemon balm, and mint.

Inhibits Diarrhea. Garlic, thyme, comfrey, savory, marjoram, sage, oregano, mint, and lemon balm.

Diuretic. Borage, lovage, and parsley.

Prevents Bad Breath. Parsley, thyme, and coriander.

Reduces Flatulence. Dill and fennel.

Spring Tonic. Chives, nasturtium, and garlic.

Lowers Blood Pressure. Garlic, chives, and lemon balm.

Reduces Inflammation. Sage and savory.

Reduces Fever. Feverfew and catnip.

Remedies Colds. Bee balm, horehound, and hyssop.

Cures Headaches. Oregano and rosemary.

If you examine ancient herbals or many modern-day herb books that emphasize herbal healing, you will probably find a lot more examples than I have just given. Many herbs are described as being "an abortifacient, an anthelmintic, antiperiodic, antipyretic, antiseptic, antispasmodic, astringent, carminative, diaphoretic, diuretic, . . ." and so forth, in long lists of properties that no one plant could possess. Furthermore, the vocabulary used in such descriptions requires frequent consultation with a good dictionary even to find out what combination of properties the herb has. I have tried to reduce the list to a few common examples.

Many herbs are not to be taken in quantity during pregnancy. Herb teas, for the most part, should be completely avoided in pregnancy, just as alcohol, tobacco, and caffeine should be, although the amounts used in seasoning food probably have no medicinal effect. (Remember that tobacco, coffee, and real tea are just plant products, too; being natural is no guarantee of being harmless.)

HARVESTING AND DRYING HERBS

If you need specific advice about growing herbs, check in the chapters on either the perennial or annual herbs for the specific herbs. All the herbs commonly used in teas are discussed in these chapters. Bay, chamomile, comfrey, lemon balm, lovage, mint, oregano, rosemary, sages, tarragon, thyme, and winter savory are perennial herbs. Basil, caraway, chervil, coriander, cumin, dill, fennel, marjoram, and parsley are treated as annuals. Further thoughts with regard to a specific herb may be found in the chapter "Encounters with Herbs" in this book.

Dry Versus Fresh

As noted, herbs can be made into teas using fresh leaves, provided you use enough of the leaves. For medicinal purposes, some people feel that fresh leaves are better than dried ones. Sometimes I make a tea from fresh herbs to help me decide if I want to go to the trouble of drying and blending a batch to have on hand, but for regular use, I prefer dried herbs.

One reason for preferring dried herbs is that I use a tea ball. Although both my teapots have strainers, cleaning out the tea leaves from the bottom of the pot is a chore that I do not enjoy. My wife, who tends to get stuck with such duties more often than I, hates cleaning a teapot filled with soggy leaves even more than I do. The tea ball can be filled with an appropriate amount of herbs, then dumped easily into the compost bucket with no need to reach into the pot with your hand and scrape.

A good tea ball for herb teas is the largest one you can find that will fit into the mouth of the teapot. The kind made from screening (hard to find) is probably the best, although this sort of tea ball is not very sturdy. Stainless steel tea balls last much longer—indefinitely, in fact, although the chain that is used to retrieve the ball from the pot may fall off. The reason I suggest the largest tea ball you can use is that you may want to use it for herbs. Also, even with dried herbs, I think that the results are often better if you add more herbs and steep for a shorter time.

Another reason for preferring dried herbs is that I like to have a cup of tea with breakfast. It is often not convenient to go out to the herb garden to pick fresh herbs first thing in the morning.

Of course, some of the herbs most useful for teas are generally not available in the winter in a fresh form. While a gardener with a greenhouse might manage to have lemon balm, chamomile, and mints on hand all winter, these herbs present some problems as houseplants, especially chamomile. Even if chamomile were grown in the house, it would be hard to get it to blossom in the winter.

But the most important reason for using dried herbs is that I can make a big batch at a time and know what I am getting when I make a cup of tea. A batch of dried herbs can be adjusted several times by adding a bit of this or a lot of that until you get a blend you like. (Pure herb teas may have medicinal properties, but I find that I much prefer the blends.) The final product can be stored in a large jar sealed with a tight lid or in a canister.

It is true that when you make the next batch of tea, you may have forgotten how the previous one was put together. Therefore, it is a good idea to list the ingredients so that you repeat the same blend of tea. I generally forget to do this, however.

Smaller sealed jars can be used to hold leftover dried herbs to use in the next blend. The same dried herbs can be used in cooking when for some reason the fresh or frozen herbs are not available.

There is no difference between the dried herbs used in teas and those used in flavoring food. Dried herbs purchased in supermarkets as flavorings, however, may not be entirely suitable for making teas, for they may be powdered. Even the purchased herbs that are supposed to be whole leaves are often partially crushed. Powdered and crushed herbs tend to float about in the tea, making it cloudy and even gritty. The nearer you can get to whole leaves, the better.

Dried herbs will keep for a long time in a sealed jar, especially if the jar is stored in a dark place or at least out of direct sunlight. The flavor does gradually diminish, however. It is best to plan to have enough dried whole leaves for the whole period from midsummer to midsummer, but you should dry and prepare teas every year, rather than try to carry them over from year to year.

Harvesting Herbs

Herbs for drying should be harvested just before the plant is ready to flower, since the flavor is strongest at that time. If you also snip off the flower buds at the same time, then you can often make an additional harvest at a later time, also just before flowering. While you might not want to repeat this procedure too often with a perennial herb, it can often be used three or four times over the summer (perhaps more with some herbs that are fast growing, such as basil). Of course, if you want seeds from the herb, you have to let it flower. If the seeds are the most important part of the herb to you, it is just as well not to inhibit flowering by taking the leaves at all. Either grow two batches of the herb—one for leaves and one for seeds—or forego the leaves.

For the herbs that I use in a lot of teas, I have developed several different approaches. The perennials present various habits of growth, each of which must be dealt with in its own way. The directions that follow apply to harvesting for any form of storage, freezing, drying, or making into a sauce or vinegar, so I am providing harvest notes for plants that you would be unlikely to dry, such as chives, which are much better frozen.

In general, the best harvesting tool is a pair of scissors. I use the kind of scissors intended for cutting hair, which work just as well on herbs.

Although lemon balm is a perennial, it is so vigorous I generally cut the plant off about a third of the way from its base, drying the entire top two-thirds of the plant. It will come back, even if you are not sure that you want it to. Mints are equally aggressive, and there are generally more plants around than you want. I take the whole plant from its base. Oregano that has been in place a while develops numerous branches from a central point. While they may be connected underground, essentially each branch can be treated as a separate plant, so I remove a number of branches at the base level, leaving about half of them behind to flower and to preserve the plant.

Tarragon can be treated in the same way as oregano. Thyme and winter savory are pruned back to about two-thirds of their original growth, since they are less vigorous than other members of the mint family (especially thyme). Sage is even less secure than thyme, and also it has bigger leaves. I just pick about a third of the leaves, being careful to distribute the picking so that each branch retains two-thirds of its leaves. Bay gets a similar treatment to sage, with rather more leaves left and fewer picked. Rosemary is pruned, but not so extensively as thyme. Chives, on the other hand, seem to do better if they are clipped almost to ground level, while lovage is so large that an adequate supply for most purposes can be obtained from cutting off a few branches.

Chamomile is in a class by itself, of course. You just harvest and dry the flower heads.

Many of the annuals are in the carrot family—parsley, dill, fennel, coriander, cumin, chervil, and caraway, for instance. Since these are grown in quantity, I remove whole plants or, in the cases where there are many branches coming from a central point, such as parsely, just the outside branches. Since parsely is really a biennial, if you want to dry it or freeze it (it is not very good dried), you should not wait until just before the flowers form, but harvest in the first year. Basil is an annual mint, but I like to get several harvests from it, so I just snip off the top fifth or so of each branch, then dry the leaves separately.

If you are harvesting seeds, it is a good idea to cut each seed head so that it falls directly into a paper bag. Otherwise, the seed heads are likely to lose lightly attached seeds. (Losing seeds this way is called *shattering* by gardeners, for some unknown reason.) Then the seeds can be removed by shaking the bag, and finally by lifting out the heads and letting the seeds fall into the bag.

Drying Herbs

Some people separate the leaves from the branches with all herbs they are going to dry, then dry just the leaves. Where I harvest entire branches or whole plants, I prefer to dry first, then remove the leaves. This is especially true if the leaves are tiny, as is the case with most herbs. For plants such as sage or basil, for which the leaves are a substantial size, I place the leaves on a screen to dry. Since I cut the branches of basil, I remove the leaves from the branches before drying.

Most people wash the leaves before drying, to eliminate dust. I do not have a particularly dusty garden, so I sometimes eliminate this step if the leaves appear to be clean when they are harvested. If the leaves are washed, it is important to wipe off any excess water and to start the drying process as soon as possible. The same considerations apply to washing whole branches or plants, although they are even less likely to be dusty or to be easy to dry if washed.

My wife is fond of drying a few branches of oregano or tarragon by hanging them from hooks or strings in the kitchen. It looks very attractive, and the herbs dry in fairly short order, but there are some problems with this method. For one thing, the herbs get a bit dusty. The biggest problem is that they look so attractive that we never take them down and store them in jars. In fact, we never use them at all. They become decoration—nice, but not very practical.

To dry an entire plant or a large branch of a plant, the best method I have found is to poke the stem through the bottom of a bag, tie a string to the stem, and suspend the plant-in-a-bag in a very warm place. The point of the bag is to keep dust off the herbs and yet still keep air circulating around the herbs, so the bag should be large enough that the herb branch is not crowded.

In the middle of the summer, when I dry herbs, my attic is a perfect, very warm place. Plants are suitably dry within a few days, and they retain their green or gray-green color. Lacking a hot summer attic, you can also dry herbs in a low oven. Lay the branches directly across the oven racks for the best circulation. They will dry in several hours in a 150°F oven. Leave the oven door open to permit the moisture to escape. (This can be pretty uncomfortable on a hot summer day, however.) If the weather is suitable, you can also dry herbs in the sun. In that case, it is best to use the screen method described below for drying leaves.

Small branches and clippings or individual leaves can best be dried on a screen, unless they are to be dried in the oven. In the oven, the herbs can be scattered in one layer over a piece of brown paper or foil with slits cut in it to allow the air to circulate. For attic or outdoor drying, a single layer of herbs on an old window screen permits the air to circulate around the herbs and speeds drying. There is still the matter of dust to deal with. In the attic, I put cheesecloth over the herbs. The same idea can be used outdoors, provided the cheesecloth is weighted at the corners so the wind does not blow it or the herbs away. Note that time of drying in the sun will vary considerably, depending on the weather and humidity.

The herbs are dry, no matter where you dry them, when they crumble easily and crinkle when you crush them. At that point you should strip the leaves and store them in tight containers. Do not crumble the leaves until you are ready to use the herbs in a tea blend or in cooking. The herbs keep their flavor better when the leaves are left whole.

If you dry whole branches of herbs as I do, you will discover that it is somewhat messy to get the dried leaves separated from the stems. Of course, for teas, this is not so important as it is for flavoring, since the dried stems will contribute something to the flavor of the tea, but will not get into the part you are consuming. For flavoring foods, however, it is important to use just the leaves, or you may find that you are spearing the inside of your mouth with a piece of stem. Even for teas, it is a good idea to get rid of the stems, since they do not readily crumble and therefore contribute too much to the bulk. In a tea ball, this can result in dilute tea.

Since removing the leaves is messy, a good way to do it is on a spread-out newspaper. You can pile the stems on one corner of the newspaper and the leaves on another if you are working on a table. I like to work on my lap and watch television while I am separating leaves and stems. Something that does not require constant looking at the screen works best, such as television news or an old movie that is interrupted by a lot of commercials. If you are a football or baseball fan, that is perfect, since football and baseball both have long pauses between actions. By listening to the announcer, you will know when you have to look away from the herbs to see the action.

Of course, if you are working on your lap, it is impossible to pile the leaves and stems in separate piles on the newspaper. Both piles tend to slide to the center of the paper. One good method is to have a paper grocery bag next to your chair. Allow the leaves to slide to the center of the paper, while you toss the stems into the bag. When you have enough leaves on the paper, you can fold the newspaper to guide the leaves into a jar or canister for storage.

There is one limited use for the stems of some of the herbs that you have collected. If you are grilling meat, chicken, or fish on an open fire, a handful of dried herb stems at the end of the grilling period can impart a slight flavor to the food. This use is limited because the flavor is really quite feeble. You can get a better effect by repeating the process several times throughout the grilling period. Also, although the most smoke is produced when the herb stems are actually in flame, you do not want to singe the food. A few small handfuls will therefore do better than throwing in a big bundle of stems.

Good herbs to use for flavoring in this way are the same ones you would use in a marinade to flavor the food being grilled or that you would apply directly to the meat, chicken, or fish: rosemary, thyme, fennel, dill, oregano, and so forth. The more woody the stems are, the better the grilling system works, because woody stems such as rosemary or thyme form a kind of charcoal after the initial burning, which adds to the flavor.

MAKING TEA

The American people have sadly become accustomed to making tea by dunking a bag in a cup of hot water or by putting a teaspoonful of powdered chemicals in the cup and adding hot water. Of course, they probably know that this is the wrong way to make tea, even though it is very convenient. While I have yet to see any powdered instant herbal tea, I suspect that some entrepreneur either has produced it or is working on it in the basement now.

I had high hopes when I visited England that I would find real tea properly made. Sad to say, the English like convenience just as much as Americans do. There is a slight variation, however. At home, the English use teapot-size bags to make a potful of tea at a time. Unfortunately, these large bags are not equipped with strings, so there is no way to remove the bag conveniently when the tea is done. I suppose that the assumption is that all of the tea will be poured from the pot, but that does not always happen. Real tea, when left to soak, releases the bitter tannins that overwhelm the flavor. Fortunately, most herbs are low in tannins, so herb teas can be steeped for longer than real tea to obtain a stronger flavor without getting a shock when you take your first sip. Steeping herb teas too long is not recommended, however, because the active ingredients may turn out to be more active than you want them to be (see "Teas as Medicine" earlier in this chapter for some of the possible results).

People who are serious about tea of any kind are concerned as much with the water as they are with the plant materials that are infused into the water to make the tea. Although using bottled water for herb teas would seem to be extreme, the water does affect the flavor of the infusion. Unless you do use bottled water, however, it is difficult to use anything but tap water in making tea. How the tap water is handled affects the flavor also, and that is easier to control.

When the water has just come from the tap, it has a lot of oxygen in it, a good quality in making tea. On the other hand, if the water sits around for a while, it loses the chlorine that may have been added, an effect also to be desired. Unless your water supply is unchlorinated, these considerations are at odds with each other. I have decided that I prefer the fresh, chlorinated water to the water that has been around for a while, emitting chlorine. Therefore, I always start each pot of tea with fresh, cold water. Cold water is to be preferred because it has more oxygen, and therefore more "life." I heat the water just to boiling and make the tea in the pot. If you let the water actually boil, you will have lost the oxygen. I think—but I do not know—that much of the chlorine is lost in heating the water.

Some people believe that you should go further to preserve the quality of the water. They steep the tea in water direct from the hot-water tap, with no boiling. Perhaps this is an acquired taste. I have tried it and found the tea produced to be insipid.

Tastes vary, but I like to steep my "standard" blends of herb teas for about ten minutes, about twice as long as I would steep orange pekoe. If I did not use a tea ball, I could cut this time down by a couple of minutes, since the infusion takes place faster if the herbs are scattered through the tea. You need to experiment to find out for yourself how you like it. Pour off a little tea and taste it after five minutes—making sure that if the pot is quite full that you first pour away the hot water from the spout, which is not representative of the whole pot of tea. Then wait a minute or two and try again. When you are satisfied, perhaps after four or five times, you will know how long it takes to match the tea to your taste. (Remember that herbs and blends vary just as people do.) It might be a good idea to go slightly beyond the way you like it the first time, just to be sure that you do not want a stronger tea.

If you are using the herbs in tea, a rounded teaspoon of dried herbs per cup of tea is about right. Of course, if you are making a pot of tea, you should add an additional teaspoonful for the pot. Also, if you are in a hurry, you can use somewhat greater amounts of dried herbs and steep the tea a shorter time.

Herb teas are good iced as well as hot. You may want to make more tea than you need, saving the remainder of the tea to have iced later in the day.

Many people like to sweeten all tea, including herb teas. Honey is often recommended as a sweetener, and it makes a good one. Sometimes, however, people assume that because honey is natural and refined sugar is processed, that honey is nutritionally much superior to refined sugar. While there are trace amounts of vitamins and minerals in honey that are not also found in refined sugar, the amounts are far too small to make much of a nutritional difference. The real advantage of honey is that it is sweeter than sugar. (Honey's sweetener is fructose, a sweeter compound than sucrose, the sweetener in sugar; in fact, refined sugar is all sucrose.) Since honey is sweeter, you can get the same effect by using less of it, which is nutritionally advantageous because it means fewer calories from a source that does not also contribute much in the way of vitamins and minerals and nothing in the way of proteins, fats, or complex carbohydrates. Using less honey means that you can add more nutritional foods to your diet without excess calories.

Unfortunately, my observation of people who sweeten herb teas suggests to me that they use just as much honey as they would sugar. The result is a very sweet tea with no advantage over using sugar. If you like your tea sweet, by all means use honey, but try to get by with as little as possible to obtain a flavor you like.

Although many people add milk or cream to real tea, it is not common to do so with herb tea. Nutritionally, that is probably sound, since most people get too much milk fat in their diet as it is.

Since I always drink my tea, real or herb, without sugar or milk (although sometimes with a little lemon), I cannot comment very much on how milk or honey affects the flavor. Lemon in herb teas is unnecessary, of course, if they contain such herbs as lemon balm or lemon verbena (although using real lemon would add some vitamin C and not detract from the lemon flavor of the herbs).

Chapter 5
The Practical Indoor Herbs

Women's magazines are fond of showing pictures of kitchens in which the windowsill is graced with a veritable herb garden. The accompanying article suggests that this effect is both easy to achieve and handy for the cook. Indeed, there are all the fresh herbs you might ever want, shown in glorious color, and you do not even have to step outside to get them.

Garden stores and even supermarkets sell kits that supposedly enable you to achieve the result pictured in the magazines. Such kits are also graced with photographs showing a kitchen window all hung about with chives, thyme, marjoram, dill, basil, parsley, rosemary, and sage. The typical kit consists of seeds for all of these, along with pots and some starting soil. There may even be a wire arrangement for hanging the tiny pots from the window.

Sad to say, the effect pictured in the women's magazines or on the packaged herb kits generally cannot be achieved. There are so many practical difficulties in the way that I scarcely know where to begin. Suffice it to say that it is likely that the photographs were not made in a real kitchen, and that the herbs shown were most likely grown elsewhere and simply carried in for the picture. (Perhaps you have wondered how fairly dark restaurants can be hung all about with potted plants. The answer is that the plants are rented. After a few weeks in the restaurant, the plant renter takes the plants from the restaurant and returns them to a healthy environment. New plants are put in the restaurant. In another few weeks, the process is repeated. Kitchen herbs gardens are essentially rented as well.)

Despite the problems with growing herbs in the kitchen, most herbs can be grown in the house, at least for a while. Even the herbs that do fairly well indoors, however, are likely to last for a shorter time than other houseplants. If the conditions are right, all herbs can be grown indoors for the winter, and in northern climates bay and rosemary *must* be taken in for the winter.

Kitchens are unlikely places for indoor growing even for over-wintering. Remember that most herbs want a lot of sunshine. Unless the kitchen has a south-facing window, it is better to keep your herbs in another room. Furthermore, kitchens have stoves in them. If the stove is electric, the only problem would be that the herbs might find the heat too drying, but the fumes from gas stoves tend to be damaging to plants, especially to some of the herbs.

The life cycles of herbs are adjusted to being outdoors. Some herbs require a cool period or even cold weather to complete their life cycle properly—notably chives and tarragon, which ought to freeze once a year. Members of the mint family tend to die back and spring up a little distance (or a great distance) away. This is hard to do in a pot.

The pots sold in herb kits for hanging in a kitchen window are too small for almost all herbs. I am not just referring to the giant herbs such as lovage or comfrey. A pot that is 2 or 3 inches in diameter and about the same depth is too small for any herb except possibly for a clump of chives. Even a herb that does not show a lot of green above the surface of the soil may have a long taproot, as the members of the carrot family do. Unless you have a suitable shelf made specially for the purpose, the chances are good that you do not have the space to put large-enough pots for herbs in your kitchen. The smallest herb pot should be 4 inches in diameter, but larger herbs require larger containers.

Having said all of this, I want to reiterate that it *is* possible to grow herbs indoors—provided you have suitable pots, good light, and even and low heat. Do not expect the same results as you would get from plants grown outside. The following is a brief analysis of the possibilities for each of the major herbs. The following discussion deals with permanent indoor plantings, started for that purpose. A little later in this chapter, I deal with the related but different question of bringing herbs from the garden inside for the winter.

Basil. Since Keats wrote a well-known poem about a pot of basil, it is not entirely unexpected that basil can be grown indoors. For one thing, you are likely to have better results indoors with tropical or semitropical plants than with those from the North because the interiors of most homes are hotter than the air outside, especially if the herb is kept in a sunny window. (Remember, however, that the Mediterranean herbs, while they like a lot of sunlight, also are bred to like a more humid climate than is found inside the house; such herbs do better if misted daily.) The only special consideration for basil is to use one of the smaller varieties unless you have a place for a large pot or tub. Since the basil sold as started plants in garden stores tends to be the standard size (except the Dark Opal variety, which sometimes is sold as a plant), it is safer to purchase seeds of a dwarf variety and start it yourself.

Bay. Bay does well indoors up to a point. If you start with a very small plant, you might want to keep it indoors until it is large enough to cope, even if you plan to leave the bay outdoors all the time (in the South; it must be taken inside in the North). Although bay grows very slowly, it does eventually grow to be a quite large plant. If you start it in a small pot, you might need to keep transplanting it every few years until it is in a tub. If at all possible, bay should spend the summers outdoors, for better growth.

Caraway. If you grow caraway for the seeds, you will have little luck growing the plant indoors. Not only do most herbs set fewer (or no) seeds in the house, but also caraway is a biennial that expects to encounter a cold winter between its first and second years. Since the seed comes in the second year, the caraway that is disappointed by lack of winter is unlikely to go to seed at all.

Chamomile. I have never heard of chamomile being grown inside and for practical purposes (tea), you would have to grow a lot more than a single plant.

Chervil. Chervil is on most list of herbs that can be grown indoors, especially since it can take a little less sunlight than some of the other herbs. Given the problems I have had growing chervil outdoors, perhaps I should give it a try indoors.

Chives. Often grown inside, and even available in potted form in supermarkets, chives do well in the house, although they are not so large as chives grown outdoors. Because chives miss their natural life cycle (which includes being frozen in the winter) indoors, do not expect a pot of chives that stays indoors all the time to have a long life.

Comfrey. Comfrey is too big for practical growing in the house.

Coriander. Like most of the members of the carrot family, coriander can be grown inside for its leaves, although it will not do so well as outdoor coriander.

Cumin. Plants grown primarily for their seeds are not practical indoors.

Dill. If grown for its leaves, dill is a suitable indoor plant, although not long-lasting.

Egyptian Onions. There would not be much point to growing Egyptian onions indoors.

Fennel. Too big for most people, fennel, however, would be dwarfed somewhat by growing in a pot.

Garlic. There is no point to growing garlic for the cloves, but an indoor garlic plant could provide a small amount of garlic flavor if you snip its leaves. If you have no garden space outdoors at all, however, it is probably better to buy packaged garlic at the supermarket.

Lemon Balm. Can be grown indoors and does not require as much sun as some of the other herbs.

Lovage. Lovage, like comfrey, is too big to be grown indoors.

Marjoram. Often grown indoors, marjoram might surprise you by being a perennial.

Mint. Most of the mints can be grown indoors provided the soil is kept fairly moist. Also, they do not need quite so much light as the other herbs.

Nasturtium. If it gets sufficient light but not too much heat, a nasturtium can be grown indoors. In the house, nasturtium prefers the nighttime temperature to be in the 40s. That is too cold for most kitchens or bedrooms.

Oregano. Like its look-alike, marjoram, oregano is often grown indoors. You will get more leaves and a longer life from either plant if you prevent it from flowering.

Parsley. While parsley is perhaps the most common indoor herb, it never does so well in the house as parsley growing outside (perhaps because of the taproot problem). Also, parsley does not produce very well indoors. One solution is to grow a number of plants together in the same pot. The result is more attractive than a single plant, and you have a chance of getting enough parsley for cooking. While parsley needs a lot of sunlight, temperatures should be fairly cool for best growth.

Rosemary. Rosemary makes an excellent indoor plant, requiring only good care, especially with regard to watering. Too much or too little water and the plant will suddenly die. Rosemary seems to do best in a pot that is the size of its roots, rather than in a large tub. Rosemary grows quite slowly indoors. That could be a problem if you are using a lot of its leaves for flavoring. Summers outside will generally take care of this problem, however.

Sage. Sage does not do well in the house. Some herb gardeners solve this problem by growing pineapple sage inside, but pineapple sage is not a culinary substitute for garden sage. (Pineapple sage is a better-looking plant, however.)

Tarragon. Tarragon grows reasonably well indoors. You may run into conflicting advice from different sources on getting it started indoors. Since tarragon does not set seed, you must start with root divisions, probably from a plant growing outdoors. There are differing opinions on whether it is better to take the divisions in the spring or early summer or to take the divisions in the fall and freeze the plant in its pot before bringing it in the house. This conflict in ideas simply represents two different ways to solve the same problem (which is that tarragon is supposed to die back in the winter). If it is persuaded not to die back, it will do very poorly. My belief is that if you want tarragon in the house during the late winter, you should let it freeze in the fall and then wait for it to resprout. It will generally be back in good shape by mid-February, although there will be little or no tarragon from the time it is frozen until then. The other method would be better for someone who wants tarragon but has no garden space at all. If you want indoor tarragon for the whole winter, you might be better off following both procedures. By the time the division gathered in the spring is beginning to fade from lack of freezing, the one gathered in the fall should be working its way back to life.

Thyme. If given plenty of light and careful watering, thyme does well indoors. The soil should never be more than moist and should be allowed to dry out between waterings.

Winter Savory. Grows well indoors. Treat it like thyme, but do not use too much of it during the winter months. Unlike thyme, winter savory tends to lose its leaves in the winter when it is outdoors, and it correspondingly grows very slowly indoors in the winter (although keeping the leaves).

LIGHT FOR GROWING

All of these considerations apply primarily to growing herbs in pots in a living room or sun-room. If you have a greenhouse or can grow a small bed of herbs in a specially constructed indoor planter, you can probably do better than indicated in the listings on pages 86, 87, and 88. For example, herbs in a planter will usually have more depth of soil, so the carrot cousins will have room for their taproots.

Furthermore, a special planter may have fluorescent lights. It is difficult, outside of a greenhouse or sun-room, to get the necessary 4 or 5 hours of sunlight that most herbs need. You need to use more exposure time with fluorescent lights than is required for direct sunlight, but the extra exposure is easy to achieve. For most herbs, the right amount of time is about 12 hours of light from fluorescent bulbs each day, but that is only an approximation. If you turn on the lights when you get up and turn them off when you go to bed, the herbs will be satisfied.

Incandescent lights (that is, ordinary light bulbs) do not have the same effect, although they make a minor contribution to the herbs' light needs. The problem is that the parts of the spectrum that plants use in photosynthesis are not well represented in the spectrum of light from an incandescent bulb. Also, an incandescent bulb that is close to the herbs will tend to dry them out because it is much hotter than a fluorescent bulb.

Although regular fluorescent bulbs have a better spectrum than incandescent lights, the spectrum from regular fluorescents is still far from perfect. At most garden stores you can buy special fluorescents that have been coated to produce a good spectrum for growing plants, but they are very expensive. A better idea is to combine two kinds of inexpensive fluorescents because most planters that use fluorescents use at least two bulbs. Fluorescent bulbs come in the regular and in the cool white varieties, as well as the special bulbs for growing plants. Neither the regular type or the cool white by itself has the exact spectrum plants need, but the combination does quite well. Nothing but sunlight has exactly the right spectrum, however, which is why herbs under fluorescents require to or three times as long in the light as they need in the sun.

OTHER PROBLEMS

Most of the problems that herbs have come from the fact that they are adapted to living in an environment that is not so hot, so dry, so constant, nor so confined as a pot in a house. Furthermore, as indicated on pages 86, 87, and 88, not all herbs have the same requirements. There are a few constants, however.

Although the Mediterranean herbs are from what we think of as a warm climate, it is not so hot as many people's houses, either in the winter or in the summer. Certainly, a room in which herbs are grown ought not have a temperature much higher than 68°F if possible. Slightly warmer in the daytime is all right so long as the temperature is reduced at night. I keep my indoor herbs in my office; it might be too warm during the day in the winter but it is reasonably cool most of the summer. Furthermore, the heat in the office is turned off at night, so the herbs have a chance to cool down. If you have a room that corresponds to the use pattern of my office, it is a good room for the herbs as far as temperature goes.

Air conditioning in the summer is not too hard on herbs, so long as the plants are not in the draft from the air conditioner. Herbs do not appreciate drafts any more than people do.

Low humidity is also a problem, especially in the winter, but it is easier to deal with than heat. Herbs will do better if misted when they are in a dry house. You can make an inexpensive mister from a used bottle of spray cleanser provided you make sure that all the cleanser has been rinsed out of the bottle. A fine spray of water over all the leaves not only makes the herb feel better but also improves its looks. The Mediterranean herbs—basil, bay, chervil, coriander, lemon balm, marjoram, oregano, rosemary, and thyme—are especially pleased with this kind of treatment.

Insect pests may be more of a problem in the house than outdoors, especially if there are other plants that harbor white flies, red spiders, green aphids, or any of the other multicolored pests of houseplants. Since you are using the herbs for culinary purposes, it is imperative not to spray the leaves with a poison. Some folks think that a mixture of garlic and red pepper, made into an infusion, will handle anything (and it certainly will not be harmful to your health). Although it might not improve the herb's flavor, dipping the plant in a soap-and-water solution might be a more powerful deterrent than garlic and pepper, although I would be sure that I was using real soap, not a detergent, and I would rinse the plant very well. Actually, I have never had a problem with insects or plant disease so severe that I did anything about it at all.

BRINGING HERBS IN FOR THE WINTER

Although rosemary and bay are the only two herbs (in the basic list) that need to come in for the winter, you may want to keep herbs growing indoors during the cold months rather than relying on dried or frozen herbs. If you have a suitable place to keep the herbs, this is really much better than using preserved herbs. With the exception of those herbs that are grown in pots or tubs, as bay and rosemary should be, however, the method of obtaining fresh herbs is more complicated than simply carrying the herbs inside the house.

There are, however, a number of herbs that can be grown successfully in tubs and that can just be carried indoors in the winter like bay and rosemary. Here are some of the more common kinds.

Curry. Not the same as curry powder and not the same as the curry leaf tree, this herb is grown as much for its looks as for the curry flavor of its leaves. Reportedly it can survive mild winters outdoors.

Lemon Verbena. Lemon verbena is a pleasant, old-fashioned plant whose leaves are often used for lemon flavoring in teas. I have had one for years, which I have always taken in the house at the first hint of frost. But all its leaves dried up and shriveled each year soon after I brought it in. I thought that it was something I was doing wrong about the water or that red spiders, to which lemon verbena is extremely vulnerable, were getting it. Finally I learned that all the dried leaves were not the result of something I was doing wrong. Lemon verbena, although a tropical plant, is basically deciduous. It is suppose to lose its leaves in the winter. In the house, where there is no wind, the leaves do not fall off, making it a scraggly plant indeed. A few green leaves start to emerge at the same time as the others are dying, and by February, there will be quite a bit of new growth. The plant improves even more rapidly if you cut it back drastically at that time. When the plant is returned to its spot outside, it will soon be itself again.

Pineapple Sage. Somehow it never occurred to me that a sage would be tender, so the first pineapple sage I had succumbed to the first light frost. Resolve: the next one goes in a tub and comes inside in the winter.

Golden Thyme. Like pineapple sage, golden thyme is a better decoration than a seasoning.

Aloe. Aloe is even more tender than other tender perennials, so most people grow it as a houseplant. It can be kept outdoors in its pot when the temperature is above 50°F at night (that is, when tomatoes are growing). Aloe is valued for its juice, which seems to help burns heal.

Lavender. Not all varieties of lavender need to be brought in during the winter, but some do. The problem is that lavender is quite variable from plant to plant. Also, what is fringed lavender to one gardener is French or Spanish lavender to another. The kind that can stay outdoors is generally known as English lavender, but this species is quite variable also. To make sure you have a hardy lavender, your plant should be started from a cutting of a hardy lavender. Otherwise—it's the tub.

Scented Geraniums. These plants are normally called geraniums, but due to some botanical mix-up at some time in the past, the *Geranium* is really another genus. Modern gardeners are gradually learning to call the scented geraniums by their genus name, *Pelargonium,* but herb gardeners are old-fashioned. The scented geraniums make excellent tub plants.

Lemon Grass. Lemon grass is a common ingredient in commercial herb teas and an important element in Indian and Indonesian cooking. Although I have never seen it available in the United States, if you can get it, grow it in a tub. Since it is a tropical plant, rather than a Mediterranean or subtropical herb, it does best in really hot and humid weather. A humid greenhouse would be better than outdoors, except on the most uncomfortable days of the summer for humans, conditions that suit lemon grass fine.

The problem with plants that are *not* grown in tubs (as all the above list should be) is that most of the herbs are too old by the end of the summer to be transplanted to pots or tubs for indoor use. Annuals are nearing their natural demise, while perennials will have grown large root systems. It is far better to handle all the nontubbed plants as if you were starting over. For many of the plants, the best way to continue to have fresh herbs in the winter is to start some in the fall. This group includes all the annuals, as well as a few other plants that start readily and successfully from seed: basil, chervil, dill, fennel, marjoram, nasturtium, parsley, and thyme.

You can do better with some plants by making a root division or by taking a small plant that has formed as an offshoot. Among the plants for which this is the preferred approach are chives, lemon balm, mint, oregano, tarragon, and winter savory. If you take root divisions, be sure that you do so in time to replant the main herb long enough before winter that it gets a good hold in the soil. Also, all of these plants have a winter period bred into their system. You need to let the roots freeze before bringing the plant into the house. If you do not, the root division or the small plant will not thrive. Some think that you should wait until at least three hard freezes before bringing the plant inside.

I have had some problem getting the pots to last through the freezing process. Water in the soil expands on freezing and breaks the pot. A plastic pot does somewhat better than a clay one if the pot is left sitting on the surface of the soil, but the best solution is to use a clay pot and bury it to its lip in the soil. When the water in the pot freezes, so does the water in the soil around it, equalizing the pressure and preventing the pot from breaking. (Of course, digging the pot out of frozen soil is no easy task. You cannot count on the soil thawing after one, or even more after three, freezes. I stick to the plastic pots left on the surface and try to keep the soil in the pots fairly dry.)

Sage is a special situation because it does not transplant well, divisions are impossible, and it is extremely variable from seed. Fortunately, if you mulch a sage plant, the leaves will be perfectly usable all winter. There is really no need to bring it into the house.

WATERING AND FERTILIZING

Most of the problems with indoor herbs that are otherwise well cared for result from improper watering. While I have only lost one herb from improper watering—and that happened when it was under the care of a neighbor while we were on vacation—I am sure that various irregularities have not helped the plants in my care. Too much water or too little is easy to achieve, but exactly the right amount is a matter of trial-and-error and constant correction.

The tubbed plants that are inside for the winter are the most difficult to deal with because they are likely to be semidormant over the winter. The same applies to a lesser degree to plants that have been restarted from root divisions in the fall. Consequently, underwatering does less harm than overwatering. (The lost plant was a rosemary that was overwatered.) In my office, where the temperature is low at night but generally around 70°F in the day during the winter, the right pattern for the bay, two rosemarys, and a lemon verbena seems to be about once every five days. Since the watering chore falls on a different day of the week each week, it is hard to keep track of it. I have put it on my daily calendar, which helps.

Even if you have found the right time interval, the amount needs to be varied for the individual plants. The rosemarys, for example, should dry out between waterings. The bay should not and neither should the lemon verbena. The bay is about three times the size of the lemon verbena. Therefore, it needs more water to last the five days than the verbena does.

In the spring, as the tubbed plants are getting ready to be returned to the garden, it is a good idea to help them revive from the winter dormant period with a little fish-oil emulsion added to the water (as per directions on the bottle). Ideally, this should be done about once a week, which does not fit my five-day schedule. Less is probably better than more, so I add the fish-oil emulsion every other watering. After the tubs have been returned to the garden, the fish-oil treatment can be reduced to once a month, roughly, timing the application to match a dry spell when the tubs need watering in any case.

Outdoors, tubbed plants will dry out more quickly than the herbs that are living in the soil. Even if you do not need to water the rest of the garden because of sufficient rainfall, the herbs in pots may be drying out too much. In general, if it has not rained for five or more days, the chances are that the tubbed herbs need water.

For the other plants, watering requirements vary as well. Basil may be somewhat dormant in the winter, so it needs just enough water to keep it from wilting. Young plants that have been started from seed or from cuttings need more frequent watering than mature plants. They also need weekly fish-oil emulsion from the time they have four true leaves until they reach full size. After that, the application can be reduced to every two weeks for plants that grow satisfactorily in cool weather, such as parsley or thyme, and omitted during the winter for plants that are more tropical, such as basil, or plants that die back in winter, such as tarragon or lemon balm. If you have any doubts about your watering schedule, it is always better to underwater than to overwater.

The kind of pot the herbs are in makes a difference. Plastic or glazed pots require less frequent watering than unglazed tile or wooden tubs. If air cannot pass through the sides of the pot, water can only evaporate from the top of the pot, but unglazed or wooden sides can allow some additional evaporation (as well as more oxygen for the soil). In general, pots that breathe are preferable for herbs to pots that do not. You are much less likely to have problems with overwatering. Also, all pots need not only drain holes, but also a layer of sand or small gravel at the bottom to permit adequate drainage. A pot that does not drain will almost surely lead to overwatering.

The difference in glazed and unglazed pots is not so important as it might be because most of the water that is lost is not lost through evaporation. It is lost by a process called *transpiration*, which is loss of water vapor from the leaves of the plant. Larger plants with larger leaves will transpire more than smaller plants with smaller leaves. Waxy or stiff leaves, as on the bay, will transpire less than leaves that are soft, as on basil. All of these

94

considerations can be used in planning your watering schedule, although you will still need to experiment.

The clues to watch for to make sure that you are providing a plant with the right amount of water are in the leaves. A plant that has soft leaves, such as basil or lemon balm, will wilt—the leaves will suddenly lose erectness and perhaps even the plant will droop to the ground. This condition can be caused either by underwatering or by overwatering. (When it happens outdoors, however, it is almost always the result of not enough water.) If the leaves are stiff and the stem is woody, however, wilting will not occur. Instead, the tips of the leaves may become brown and the plant may lose some of the leaves as well. If either wilting, brown leaves, or dropping leaves starts, check the soil. If it is moist, you have been watering too much. If it is dry, you have not been watering enough. Change your schedule, the amount of water, or both.

Water meters are also available for house plants. While I have never used one, you might want to try the idea if you are inexperienced with houseplants or are having difficulty.

INDOORS VERSUS OUTDOORS

For most people who grow herbs, outdoors in the summer and indoors in the winter is the right answer. Apartment dwellers may have no choice, however, but to grow herbs in pots or tubs all year around. Even in those conditions, if there is a way to put the herbs outdoors in the summer on a balcony or fire escape, the plants will do better. Most herbs, except for those like the aloe that are desert plants, will not do as well indoors as they do outdoors. Plants will not grow to the same size, and they will tend not to flower and set seed in the house or apartment. The convenience of having herbs close to the kitchen or indoors on a rainy day is more than matched by the inconvenience of watering and fertilizing schedules and perhaps fighting off pests and diseases.

Chapter 6
Encounters with Herbs

From basil to winter savory, there are the 25 most useful herbs. They are presented with their histories and with advice for raising them as well as for using them.

BASIL

Various scientific studies have shown that companion planting does not work, so I do not believe in it—except . . .

Companion planting is the practice of growing two unrelated plants close together in the hopes that some beneficial effect produced by one of the plants will make the other plant grow better. Probably the idea first occurred to someone who noticed that one plant had a beneficial effect on some other plants around it. With that premise, people began to plant beans next to corn, rosemary or sage with the cabbages, nasturtiums among the apple trees, and basil among the tomatoes.

I strongly suspect that basil does not help tomatoes grow and that tomatoes do not help the basil; in fact, the tomatoes usually shade the basil too much, producing scraggly plants. Nevertheless, I persist each year in growing a few basil plants in my tomato patch (as well as rather more plants in the herb garden). Somehow I find the idea of basil and tomatoes as companion plants irresistible, mainly because the combination of fruits from the tomato and leaves from the basil form companions that almost everyone's taste buds find irresistible.

Basil (*Ocimum basilicum*) is the noble, tropical, and exotic member of the mint family. Basil, was popular in Europe into the Middle Ages, but then for a long time basil was somewhat out of style, except in the more southern regions. Today, fortunately, basil is an "in" herb in the United States, providing a stronger and more pleasing aroma to many dishes than could be obtained with any other flavoring or even perfume.

Basil is easy to grow if you remember its affinity with tomatoes. Simply treat basil the way you treat tomatoes. I usually buy

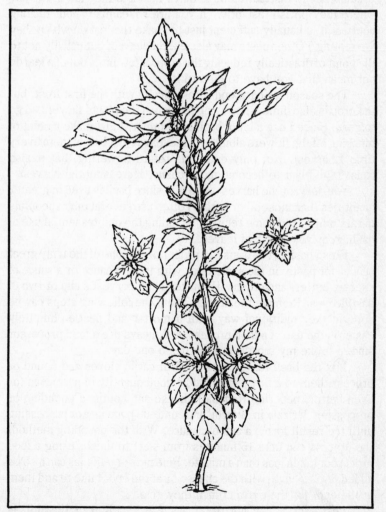

BASIL *(Ocimum basilicum)*

a flat—that is, several started plants growing in a low box—of basil about the time I set out the tomatoes, but it is also easy to start basil from seed.

Unlike most herbs, basil has problems with insect pests. I have the most trouble with Japanese beetles. My solution is to visit the plants on cool days in the summer carrying a jar of some kind of hydrocarbon, such as kerosene, turpentine, or patio-light fuel. Only an inch or so of liquid is needed in the bottom of the jar. Since the day is cool, the beetles are sluggish. Also, they are often busy mating, which tends to distract them. A quick flick and they fall in the jar, where they perish instantly. (If you are squeamish about flicking beetles, it is usually sufficient just to shake the leaf on which they are resting.) Other pests may also eat the leaves, but usually not to the point of drastically reducing the crop. A few bites out of a leaf do not mean that you have to discard it.

The season for basil ends dramatically with the first frost, but the crop is also diminished along the way if the plants flower and go to seed. Since I use a lot of basil all summer, I just make a point of pinching off the flowers along with the leaves just below them every time I harvest. Not only does this retard flowering, but it also causes the plant to become more bushy, increasing the harvest.

You do want the harvest to be big, since basil is used in greater quantities than most other herbs. I often use several tablespoonfuls in ratatouille, and some recipes, including the quintessential use of basil, require cupfuls of leaves.

Fresh basil is the basis of a proper pesto, one of the truly great sauces for pasta, in the same class with tomato sauce or a sauce of cheese, butter, and cream. To make pesto, harvest a cup or two of basil leaves. Remove the stems. Then, the following steps can be done in the traditional way with a mortar and pestle. Infinitely easier is the use of a food processor. I always use a food processor since I broke my mortar making pesto one day.

Mix the basil leaves with several garlic cloves and pound or process them to a fine puree. Add a good quantity of parmesan (or even better, pecorino Romano) cheese and continue pounding or processing. Drizzle in olive oil and continue pounding or processing until the result forms a smooth sauce. With the pounding method, the process can take 15 minutes from start to finish; using a food processor takes less than a minute. Pine nuts or pignolas can also be added, either along with the cheese or at the end. I like to add them at the end, for the extra crunch they give.

Pesto served on hot pasta, such as capellini or linguini, is terrific. Pesto added to tortellini and allowed to cool to room temperature is also terrific, and it makes a good appetizer and a good luncheon salad.

BAY

No herb is harder to locate in the United States—at least in the Northeast—than the bay, *Lauris nobilis;* but it is worth the search. After missing some that were advertised in a Manhattan plant store, I finally found mine at a plant sale run annually to support the Brooklyn Botanical Gardens. It was a tiny plant, only two or three leaves on a matchstick stem. The leaves, however, were unmistakably the noble bay leaves, which I had only seen dried before. I kept it in its pot for a year before I thought there were enough leaves to permit harvesting one of them without killing the plant. Today, that bay is about 3 feet tall and still growing, with hundreds of usable leaves. I have not seen a dried bay leaf for years.

The bay is one of the two or three absolutely essential herbs for the cook in the European tradition, although unknown as far as I can find out, in most other cuisines. In *The Foods of France*, Waverley Root wrote of foods cooked in wrappings of bay leaves, an extravagance unimaginable in most of the United States. A *bouquet garni*, the main seasoning for soups and stews, is simply a bay leaf plus—plus whatever fits the occasion. The bay leaf, however, is a constant.

Most food writers insist that dried bay leaves have the same flavor as fresh ones, although they deny that honor to other dried herbs. I beg to differ. Dried bay leaves have limited flavor, a flavor that is elusive to some while overpowering to others. The fresh leaves have a subtler flavor that nearly everyone can detect. With fresh leaves the flavor never overpowers food the way that dried leaves can do for those sensitive to the particular taste of dried bay.

The power of the bay was recognized early. Greek athletes were given a crown of bay leaves if they won, and Roman emperors gave themselves one as long as they could stave off the poisoners and revolting legions. Legend has it that the bay tree is the only tree never struck by lightning—and that may be true as far as I know (that is, mine has never been so struck). When mysterious diseases strike all the bay trees in the country at once, which seems to happen every few hundred years, it portends great disasters for the nation.

In its native climate, near the Mediterranean or Black seas, the bay grows to be a regular tree, 40 feet tall or more. In most of the

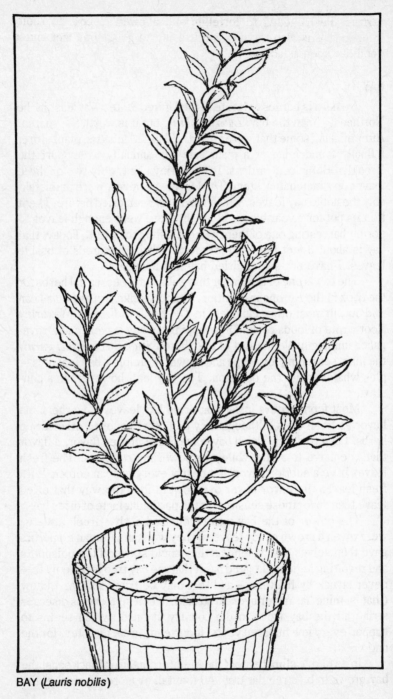

BAY (*Lauris nobilis*)

United States, however, the bay is usually grown in containers, for it does not winter well. Like the rosemary, however, it will survive the mild winters of England. At least, I was delighted to see a long row of topiaried bay trees at Hampton Court—although they were all in tubs. A bay tree in a tub does not grow to be 40 feet tall, of course. The ones at Hampton Court are each about 5 feet tall, which is about the most one can expect from a tubbed plant.

One would assume that the essential oils of the bay evolved to protect the plant from insects or other plant predators. If so, they do not do the job very well, for various insects and minor diseases attack my tree every year. The tree itself survives quite well as long as it gets a pint of water every five days and a modicum of sunlight. In the summer, when it is outdoors in the garden, it shakes of whatever ills have accumulated over the winter, puts forth a few new branches, and grows toward its maximum potted height.

If you really dote on the flavor of bay, you might try a shish kebab in which fresh bay leaves are skewered on each side of a cube of lamb or beef. For most people, however, the typical and impor- tant use of a bay leaf is to add a single leaf to a stew. The prince of stews is surely beef cooked with red wine. Here is a version that exploits the bay.

Brown the beef in a flat casserole dish made of enameled iron in a 400°F oven. When the beef is browned, remove it from the oven and take the beef from the pan, but leave the fat in (add more fat in the form of cooking oil if necessary). On top of the stove, cook sliced carrots and onions in the fat until the onions start to brown also. Put the beef back in the casserole along with a smashed clove of garlic. Sprinkle everything with pepper and flour, and cook, stirring, over a medium flame for three or four minutes.

Now add half a bottle of red wine, one or two bay leaves, and enough stock to cover the meat. Some cooks like to add a few potatoes or browned mushrooms at this point also. Simmer, either on top of the stove or in the oven, until the meat is tender. Remove the solid contents of the stew, and boil the liquid for several minutes until it thickens. You can pick out the bay leaves at this time or leave them for lucky finders. Recombine the meat, vegetables, and liquid, and serve in bowls with good bread for sopping up the liquid.

CARAWAY

I find it amazing that people sometimes confuse caraway with its southern cousin, cumin. To my mind, such sister plants as dill and fennel are more alike (although quite different in flavor). The flavor of a herb is most often affected by its essential oils, the volatile chemicals that give the herb its fragrance as well as much of its flavor. (Other factors, such as bitterness, affect the flavor as well as the oils.) Caraway and cumin do not even have the same essential oil. Nevertheless, some food writers have claimed to be unable to tell the difference between cumin and caraway.

Caraway is a very old herb in the north of Europe, while cumin is a very old herb from the south, probably from the Near East or even farther east. Caraway seeds have been found in the remains of those Swiss lake villages that were last inhabited five thousand years ago. Even today, we associate caraway with things northern, such as rye bread and sauerkraut, and associate cumin with things southern, such as cous-cous and chili (although I have seen a cous-cous recipe that calls for caraway instead of cumin, but I'm sure it was a mistranslation). In fact, the flavor that most people know as the flavor of rye bread is not the flavor of rye at all; it is the flavor of caraway.

It is true that cumin and caraway (*Carum carvi*) are closely related. Like many herbs, they are members of the carrot family. Feathery leaves and umbel-type flowers characterize all of the members of the family. Caraway is like the carrot in another way as well; it is a true biennial. (I have read that there is an annual variety that is available, but I do not know from what source.) Since caraway is usually grown for its seeds, you have to wait two years for the harvest. If you cannot wait, it is possible to eat the whole plant, including the carrotlike root, as a vegetable, but I have never felt the inclination to try it. Several authorities recommend adding the greens to salads, omelettes, or soup. Because caraway is green most of the year, it is available as a flavoring when a lot of other garden plants are not.

In the second year of growth, you get the flowers and then the seeds from caraway. If you fail to watch the ripening closely enough, however, you will lose the seeds, as they drop to the ground soon after ripening to a nice brown. In that case, however, you will most likely have a good chance to try again in another two years, since caraway self-sows readily.

Unlike most herbs, caraway may be attacked by insects that lodge in the seeds. Since there is no good way to tell which seeds are infected, the recommended treatment is to plunge all the seeds into boiling water for a few seconds before drying them in the sun. This will kill the insects. I hope that this information does not discourage you from ever using caraway again. After their hot-

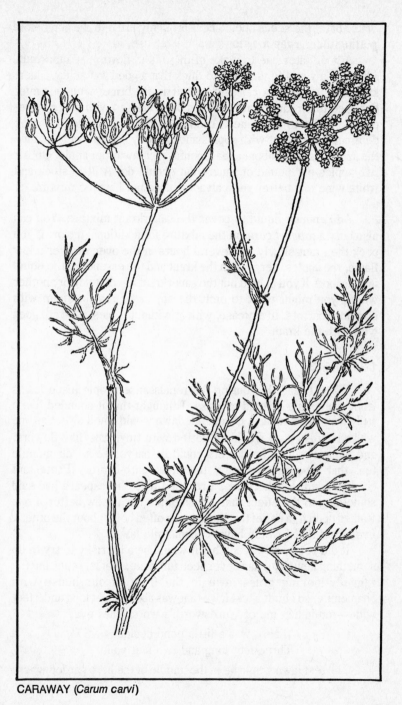

CARAWAY (*Carum carvi*)

water bath, the seeds should be thoroughly dried in the sun before putting them away for storage and later use.

A good later use to make of them is in flavoring sauerkraut. Although my mother seemed to think that a good way to eat sauerkraut was to open a can and heat it in its brine, I much prefer debrined fresh sauerkraut that has been braised with other ingredients. I like to combine a couple of different ideas, and cook debrined sauerkraut with apples and caraway seeds. Peel and dice the apples, and add about a teaspoonful of caraway per apple. One or two apples per pound of sauerkraut should do. A little stock and white wine (or, better yet, calvados) does not hurt the mixture at all.

Add enough liquid to cover the sauerkraut mixture. You can also bury a *bouquet garni* in the mixture for additional flavor. If you cook the kraut slowly for several hours in the oven or over a low flame, the apples merge with the kraut and the essence of the liquid is absorbed. If you plan to put the sauerkraut on a hot dog or another wurst, you might want to omit the apples or replace them with shredded carrots. In any case, with or without apples, mustard goes well with the kraut.

CHAMOMILE

When I read that during the renaissance people made lawns from chamomile instead of grass, I thought that it sounded like a truly marvelous idea. A chamomile lawn would smell sweet as one walked across it, it would be dotted with tiny, daisylike flowers, and, what's more, the flowers could be harvested for chamomile tea, that all-curing remedy, the nineteenth-century Protestant chicken soup. Furthermore, I recalled that Shakespeare had said something to the effect that a chamomile lawn grew better if one walked upon it (a belief that one spouse often holds about the other). I resolved that I would have a chamomile lawn.

It did seem, however, that it would be a bit risky to try to do something new that I had never seen full scale; that is, replacing the raggedy-looking grass lawn in the front of our house with chamomile, so I built a test lawn that was about 4 feet long and 2 feet wide—reminding me of Wordsworth's worst lines ever:

> There was a little pond beside,
> Three feet long and two feet wide.

The test lawn would be in the middle of the herb garden where it could be used a short walkway to visit more easily some of the other herbs.

The first problem turned out to be finding a seed packet that I could be sure was really chamomile. There are two unrelated herbs that go by the name "chamomile"; the more authentic being the species Roman chamomile (*Anthemis nobilis*). The other species, German chamomile (*Matricaria chamomilla*), is considered to be just fine for tea, but it can grow to be 1½ feet tall and is an annual

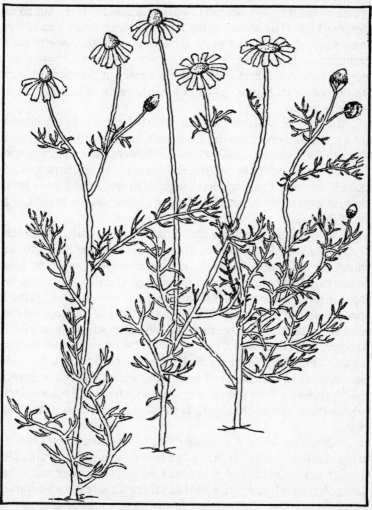

CHAMOMILE (*Anthemis nobilis*)

besides. Hardly the stuff of which lawns are made! Unfortunately, most of the seed packets that I found merely said "chamomile" and did not give either the scientific name or enough information to determine which species of chamomile was involved. Eventually, however, I found a packet that was clearly Roman chamomile, and I planted my lawn.

After the usual two or three weeks, the seeds sprouted in an irregular pattern on the little plot of land. After another couple of weeks, the weeds also began to sprout. I am not sure how Shakespeare or his friends managed to grow chamomile lawns, but he or they must have had unlimited time to spend weeding. I could grow chamomile plants, but not close enough together (because of poor germination) to make anything like a lawn, unless you counted the weeds. When the chamomile failed to make it through a tough winter one year, I gave up—after several years of failing to cope with the weeds.

Before I decided that I was not going to be able to have a lawn, I got a lot of pleasure from the chamomile anyway. For one thing, I liked to look at the small, daisylike flowers. For another, the flowers turned out to be a terrific addition to my all-purpose herb tea. In fact, after I gave up the thought of having a chamomile lawn and also gave up the chamomile, I found that my herb teas had lost a lot of their zest.

Then, a couple of years after I had seen no chamomile in the herb garden, I had a surprise. There is always a patch of ground where the dill, summer savory, and coriander has grown the year before that I do not cultivate in the spring. Usually I can count on these plants reseeding themselves over the winter. That spring I was pleased to note many small plants that I recognized as the offspring of the previous year's herbs. When my wife wanted dill for a recipe, I told her that if she did not want too much, she should use the small dill plants in the untilled part of the herb garden. She did, but complained that they had something wrong with their flavor. "Maybe they are from seed that crossed with fennel," I opined. I try to keep the fennel and dill apart, but I could have been slipshod that year.

A few days later, I was inspecting the garden, when I recognized that the "young dill" had actually been young chamomile. No wonder my wife thought there was something wrong with the flavor. Apparently seeds that had been there for at least two or three years decided that the time had finally come to germinate.

I would like to provide a recipe for the all-purpose tea, which is the only culinary use I have ever found for chamomile, but there is none. I simply harvest whatever seems tealike, dry it, and store it. Perhaps a typical mixture would be a little sage, a little mint, a lot more lemon balm, some lemon verbena, perhaps a pinch of comfrey, and as many chamomile flowers as I can get. Sometimes I throw in a few berry leaves, such as blackberry leaves or strawberry leaves, as well. The result is quite lemony, of course, but the chamomile gives it some depth.

CHERVIL

The Greek name for chervil means "herb of joy." For me, and for many other American herb gardeners, however, chervil might be more appropriately called "herb of sorrow." For some unknown reason, chervil does not grow well in the United States, although European gardeners rate it among the easiest of the herbs to grow. Perhaps we have a strain of chervil propagated in this country that is not so strong as, say, the French variety in terms of ability to withstand different soil and weather conditions. Or perhaps, there is something different about the American climate or soil that affects chervil but not other plants. Could there be some trace element missing in the United States that is commonly found in European soil? Frankly, I don't know, but I do know that out of many attempts to produce thriving stands of chervil, I have been successful only once. Therefore, my advice about growing chervil may not be so useful as it would be with regard to some other herb.

I have tried a number of different approaches to solving the chervil problem. In the beginning I planted seeds. When they did not thrive, I bought a plant. That was my successful plant, and I enjoyed chervil in my omelettes that whole summer. Thinking I had solved the problem, the following year I again bought a plant. One plant seemed sufficient, since I do not have a lot of use for chervil. However, the plant failed to thrive. In fact, it expired before I had a chance to use any of the chervil. I went back to seeds. The seeds did not germinate. I found a large and thriving plant at a local herb sale, so I bought it and carefully tended it. It lasted a while, but gradually grew smaller and eventually faded away. And so on.

On the surface, chervil (*Anthriscus cerefolium*) should not be a problem plant. It is so much like parsley that it is sometimes called French parsley, just as coriander is sometimes called Chinese parsley. The leaves of chervil are finely divided, like French

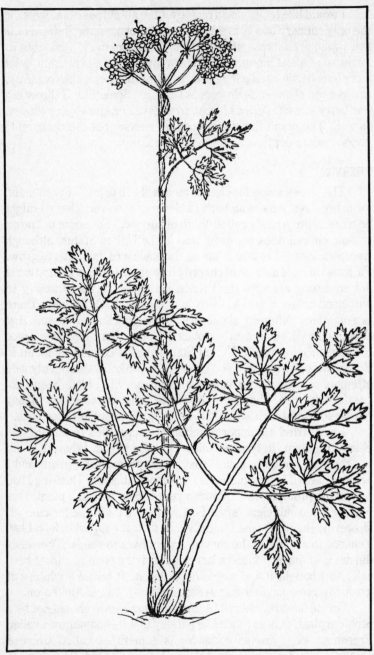

CHERVIL (*Anthriscus cerefolium*)

parsley. At first glance, chervil could be mistaken for parsley. A closer look shows that the leaves are more feathery and the overall shape of the plant is slightly different.

The flavor of chervil is considerably different; it is more assertive than that of parsley. The flavor of chervil leans toward that of tarragon; that is, there is something slightly licoricelike or aniselike to its flavor. Chervil is nowhere near as strong as tarragon, however. You can use quite a bit of chervil in combination with other herbs without having the flavor of the chervil predominate.

Chervil is definitely a worthwhile addition to your cooking, especially if you lean toward French dishes. Just as one thinks of lovage as primarily English and basil as primarily Italian, chervil is largely French in its nationality. Somehow an omelette *fines herbes* only seems truly like a French omelette when one of the "fine herbs" is chervil.

The classic *fines herbes* consists of equal portions of chervil, parsley, chives, and tarragon, but other combinations could be used. Omitting the parsley and using more of the other herbs produces a good result, as does replacing the tarragon with basil or thyme. Chervil and chives seem to me to be essential, but, lacking chives, one might use a smaller amount of shallots or the green part of scallions. For a three-egg omelette, you need about a quarter cup of chopped herbs. I also like to include several grinds of fresh black pepper, and some like to include salt as well.

Break the eggs into a small dish or measuring cup. Then begin to melt butter in an omelette pan over the highest heat. Beat the eggs lightly with the herbs and pepper. You may want to add a tablespoon of cold water for a lighter omelette, but do not add milk. (Milk or cream produces a scrambled egg, not an omelette.) As the eggs are beaten, the butter should be melting. Swirl it around the pan to coat the bottom evenly and also to coat the sides of the pan.

When the butter foams, wait until the foam begins to die down before adding the eggs, but try to get the eggs in the pan before the butter begins to brown at all. After the eggs have been added, wait a second or two, then rap the bottom of the pan on the burner to prevent sticking. Use the side of a fork to push the omelette mixture toward the center of the pan, perhaps tipping the pan to let the liquid mixture flow onto the bottom of the pan. When all the egg mixture has hardened slightly and begun to puff around the edges, either flip half the omelette over or push half over with the fork. (Often a flip needs to be completed with a push to get a neat fold.) Cook for five or six seconds, then turn out into a warmed plate. Brush the top of the omelette with butter, and enjoy.

CHIVES

One day, about 15 years ago, my wife bought a pot of chives. Although I had no idea that anything was happening, I had become a herb gardener. In the spring, the pot of chives (minus the pot, of course) was planted in the middle of what was then our vegetable and cutting garden. (A cutting garden is a place where flowers are grown, not for the purpose of seeing them outdoors, but for cutting to put in vases in the house.) The next year I was surprised to find the clump of chives already thriving in the early spring when I went out to spade the garden. Furthermore, it had grown to be much larger than the original clump.

After a couple of years, I found that the spreading patch of chives was getting in the way. I dug it up, broke it into two smaller patches, and replanted the chives in a more convenient location than the middle of what was now exclusively a vegetable garden, my wife having turned her attention to perennial flowers. As I gradually added more herbs to my vegetable garden, I realized that the situation was getting out of hand, so I started my first all-herb garden. The chives were broken into individual plants and used as the border of a stone path into the center of the garden, necessary for easy access to the herbs. There were by then enough chives left over to pot them in paper cups and give them to friends. Since chives grow well even in small pots, even the apartment dwellers I knew could benefit from having a fresh herb available on their window sills.

Today, the chive border is nearly a foot wide and in need of division again. As the earliest usable outdoor herb in the spring, the chives signal each year to my mouth and nose that winter is finally over. When they bloom, a few weeks into the late spring, the multitude of light purple blossoms is the showiest display in the herb garden, since most other herbs have small or inconspicuous blossoms.

Chives (*Allium schoenoprasum*) are the smallest and mildest member of the onion group that also includes garlic and shallots. Indeed, one of the group is the garlic chive, a plant that looks like a chive with flat leaves and white flowers, but tastes somewhat halfway between garlic and chives. The leaves of the true chive are cylindrical in cross section and quite thin, about six times as thick near the base as a blade of grass. Since chive leaves are hollow, they

110

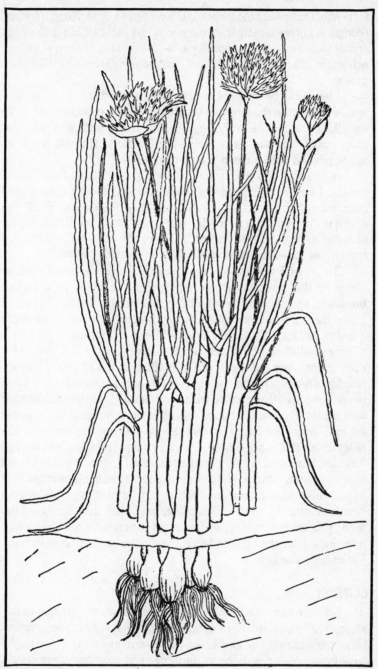

CHIVES (*Allium schoenoprasum*)

form short tubes or rings when cut for use in a dish. Nongardeners recognize chives mostly from the green rings that appear in the sour cream ladled onto baked potatoes. In the garden, however, chives are bright green spikes 1 to 2 feet long, looking somewhat like giant grass.

Chives can be frozen with some success and are often sold that way. I have often thought that the frozen-chive business must be an excellent one for the truly lazy person. Given sufficient soil, the crop would increase each year with no effort. Harvest could be accomplished with a clean rotary lawn mower.

Although I find the flavor of chives quite distinct from that of onions, I never seem to have enough scallions (young onions used mainly for their leaves) on hand. So I substitute chives. While the result is different, it is generally a happy substitution. But there are also dishes that demand chives, and no substitute will suffice. My favorite of these is simply scrambled eggs with chives.

To prepare scrambled eggs properly, I need to be inspired by company that has stayed overnight. Since it must be a festive breakfast, you allow two eggs for each guest, plus one for the pot, as in making tea. Start by melting two or three tablespoons of butter in a heavy skillet over a slow fire. While it is melting, snip into a mixing bowl about two tablespoons of chives into ⅛-inch rounds for each guest. Add the eggs and a healthy dollop of heavy cream, roughly a tablespoon for each guest. Grind in a liberal dose of black pepper and beat the mixture with a fork until all the ingredients are well mixed. By now the butter should have melted unless the fire is *too* low. Swirl the butter around the skillet to make sure that the sides of the skillet are coated as well as the bottom, and add the egg mixture. Start stirring slowly with a wooden spoon. Nothing should happen at first. After a minute or two, the eggs should slowly begin to scramble into rather small curds. If nothing happens after a couple of minutes, the fire is too low, but better that than being too high; you are not making an omelette! It may take ten minutes or even longer for the eggs to reach the desired creamy consistency. Patience is the key.

COMFREY

No herb has caused me so much confusion, in part due to my sloppy reading habits. For years, I thought that it was called *comfey*. I also thought that *comfey* was the same word as *comfy*, which might have been some reference to its large, soft-looking leaves (could they have been used for bedding?) or to the quality of the tea made

COMFREY (*Symphytim officinale*)

from the dried leaves. The idea of a comfy herb was extremely appealing, so I bought a plant and added it to the garden. It flourished. I had no clear idea what to do with it, but it was comfy just having it there.

Eventually, I noticed that I had the name wrong. Since the plant was no longer comfy in my mind, I thought that there ought to be something for which it was suited. I read that it was grown for compost. Compost? A plant just grown so that it could be thrown away? This did not make sense to me at all.

Next I found some references to comfrey tea. I chopped up some of the leaves, dried the result, and added it to a tea mixture. This seemed to be a good solution to the problem of what to do with this sprawling plant—until I read that comfrey tea might be poisonous. I stopped adding dried comfrey to teas. Since I had never tried comfrey tea alone, I did not even have any clear idea of what it tasted like.

I started looking for uses of comfrey (*Symphytim officinale*) in books on herbs. Most of them did not mention the plant at all. The common catalogs did not list the plant, either. The *Larousse Gastronomique* told me that comfrey was the name for any of several plants that could be eaten in a salad. I looked at the hairy leaves of my comfrey and decided not to try. (Comfrey is clearly related to borage, another hairy herb that I have tried in a salad—once.)

Since *officinale* is part of the scientific name, I knew that there must be some medicinal use for the plant. One of the common names is "knit-bone," which suggests a medicinal use that I find hard to believe. Comfrey did not turn up in most of the herb books I have that deal with medicinal properties, although a Colonial source is quoted in one book as suggesting a syrup of comfrey, flavored with brandy and gunpowder, for back pains.

Another possible use for comfrey turned up. It could be used to give fragrance and color to soap. All you have to do is to put a couple of tablespoons of shredded comfrey into a pint of boiling water. Steep for a half hour or so. Strain out the liquid into the top half of a double boiler and float some pure soap in it. Cook until the soap melts. Stir and pour into a flat bowl to cool. I am not sure whether it solidifies or stays liquid, since I have not tried the idea. Not only are commercial herbal soaps readily available, but I do not like them. Also, I am not sure that I would want to smell like comfrey.

Comfrey is a hardy perennial. It grows to a large size and nothing seems to bother it. While it is not exactly unattractive, it is not what I would consider a useful herb in any landscape scheme I can think of (although it is recommended for such purposes in some books). The purple flowers are too small to be suitable for a flower garden and too large to be daintily attractive, the way that, say, the flowers of thyme or rosemary are. Unless you dig up or plow under the plant, you will have it with you forever.

Europeans plant it as a cover crop in fields that lay fallow for a year or more. Then they plow it back into the soil. Apparently, its roots are especially good at bringing up nutrients from the subsoil.

With one large plant, I do not anticipate plowing it into my herb garden. After careful consideration, I have decided that I will cut it back to the ground two or three times this summer. The leaves can go into the compost. Although it seemed ridiculous at first, I am now growing a herb solely for the purpose of throwing it away.

CORIANDER

Coriander is probably the most widely used herb of all, but its use varies considerably from place to place. Europeans and East Indians mainly use the seeds. Latin Americans, probably in imitation of a plant they used in pre-Columbian days, and Chinese mainly use the leaves, although in parts of Latin America (as in ancient times in Europe), they also use the roots. I like the flavor of the leaves in moderation, but my wife gets upset if I add it to a Chinese- or Mexican-style lunch dish. Most people like the seeds, which have an entirely different flavor from the leaves. In fact, the seeds are sometimes coated with sugar and used as candy. As a result of this widespread use, coriander goes by several different names, of which "Chinese parsley" and "cilantro" are the most common.

Not only is coriander universal in geography, but also it occupies a prominent place in history and even prehistory. It was used in ancient times in the Mediterranean and Middle Eastern civilizations, being one of the herbs mentioned in an early Egyptian papyrus and in the Bible. In fact, the Hebrews noted that the manna that fell from heaven during their 40 years in the wilderness tasted rather like coriander. The Greeks and the Romans were both fond of the seeds, pure or mixed with other herbs. It became especially prominent in the late Middle Ages in Europe, after the Ottoman Turks had cut off the spices from the East.

Despite all this universality, coriander leaves are only available in specialty stores, such as Latin American *bodegas* or Chinese markets, unless you grow your own. In the summer, I always have plenty of coriander. In the winter, I do without the leaves, which must be fresh to provide their characteristic flavor. The seeds,

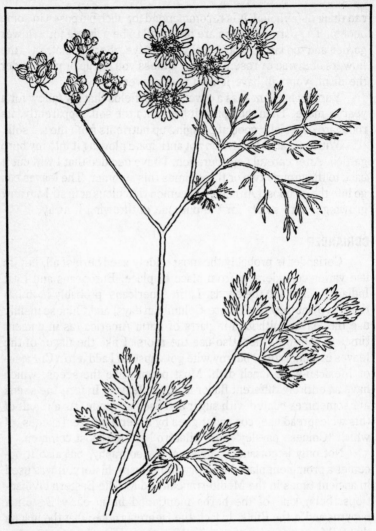

CORIANDER (*Coriandrum sativum*)

however, dry easily and may be kept all winter.

Coriander (*Coriandrum sativum*) is an easy-to-grow annual (and apparently sometimes a biennial, but that must be further south, since it does not survive even a light frost). The standard advice is to plant coriander seeds after all danger of frost has past. If you are growing coriander for the leaves, plant some more every few weeks because it quickly matures to flower and seed—at which time the leaves tend to become sparse and less flavorful. The leaves, by the way, are very peculiar. Alone among the plants I grow as vegetables or herbs, coriander has two entirely different kind of leaves; large ones that resemble Italian parsley near the base of the plant, and small ones that are somewhat spiky near the top of the plant. (Coriander also has two different kind of flowers on the same plant, but this is not so noticeable.)

Coriander will self-seed if not all of the seeds are harvested. Although the plant will not make it through the winter, the seeds will, which will provide you with your first coriander of the following spring! The fact that I have seeds overwinter each year makes me wonder about the standard advice of planting after danger of frost. It is apparent that the seeds that overwinter do not germinate until the weather is sufficiently warm. Also, it should be noted that although coriander is in the carrot family, a group notorious for poor germination, coriander seeds are the exception to that tendency.

I am partial to tacos made with coriander. A simple filling for precooked taco shells can be made from ground beef. I cook a chopped onion or two along with some chopped hot peppers in oil to start with (Hungarian wax peppers are good in tacos, Jalapeños if you prefer a hotter taco). When the onions are translucent, add garlic cloves that have been crushed and chopped. Then add the ground beef and brown it until it is cooked through. With a lid on the frying pan, pour off all the fat and discard it. Then comes the creative part—something needs to be added to the filling to make it partly tomato flavored. My son uses catsup, bottled spaghetti sauce, and chili sauce. I am apt to use anything that is at hand, including bottled barbecue sauce, tomato paste, pepper sauce, and even fresh tomatoes. Taste from time to time and experiment—or used canned taco sauce if you are inclined to want a real recipe and a predictable experience. The amount of sauce should not make the mixture at all liquid; instead, the sauce should be largely absorbed by the meat.

When you are generally satisfied with the filling, add several tablespoons of chopped coriander leaves. Set the filling aside while you heat the taco shells in a slow oven. Serve with chopped lettuce, chopped onions, chopped tomatoes, grated cheddar cheese, and warm canned taco sauce. For each taco, start with a generous amount of filling, add some sauce, then add cheese, onions, tomato, and lettuce. Top off the lettuce with a bit more sauce and enjoy.

CUMIN

For many years it never occurred to me to grow cumin. Somehow, in my mind, cumin was a spice, like nutmeg or cinnamon, a seed that grew on gigantic trees in the tropics. As I was reading a book on herbs and spices, however, I discovered that cumin was just another carrot cousin, like parsley or dill. Since I had never encountered it in any form but the ground seeds, I had let myself be misled by its rich, tropical flavor.

Since cumin is one of the flavors I use most often (in particular dishes of which I am fond; not indiscriminately), I resolved to grow my own. A little research showed me that cumin (*Cuminum cyninum*), for all its powerful flavor, is a tiny plant. In fact, it looks somewhat like a miniature dill—although it is usually compared with its northern cousin, caraway. The seeds, where the flavor is, are also tiny. The Greeks defined a miser as a person who divides everything, even cumin seeds.

Most American cooks do not realize how much cumin they use as a flavoring. When dried, the seeds become the essential ingredient in chili powder, as well as an important ingredient in most curry powders. Read the list of ingredients on the label. In fact, if an American kitchen stocks cumin at all, it is probably to use in following a recipe for some exotic dish, such as cous-cous. Chili, however, is certainly indigenous, while curry flavoring—if not actual curry—has become an important part of many typically American dishes.

Cumin is one of the herbs from the Mediterranean region, and more than many of the others, it cannot take the cold. There is good reason to believe that it was originally from warmer regions farther to the east than the Mediterranean, but it has been an important flavoring in the region around the Mediterranean since at least Biblical times. Today, however, it is little used in Europe, even though it was popular with both the ancient Greeks and the Romans.

Since cumin has a history of warm climates, in temperate climates you have to start it indoors if it is to grow large enough to produce any seeds. It is somewhat delicate to transplant, so the recommended procedure is to start clumps, rather than plants, in small pots. Then you can remove the entire clump along with all of the soil in the pot without disturbing the roots.

Because of its small size, cumin is one of the herbs that can be used for a border. There is something practical in this, as well, since it is hard to harvest the seeds from a small plant if you have to reach into the middle of a bed. Since the umbels on cumin are often tinged with pink, it makes a fairly attractive border, at least when it is in flower. When it reaches the point of becoming dried, harvest-

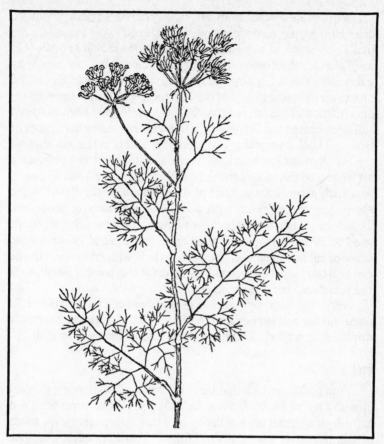

CUMIN (*Cuminum Cyninum*)

able seeds, there is not much to say for it from the looker's point of view.

Seeds dried on the plant will store and can be ground for use. The flavoring expert Tom Stobart thinks that the flavor is improved by roasting, however. As an Englishman, Stobart probably uses cumin most in curries, for which the roasting may indeed be a help. For the ordinary American cook, who most commonly uses cumin as a principal ingredient of chili powder, the dried form is more appropriate.

One of the best ways to make chili with a good depth of flavor is to follow a procedure I learned from the great English food writer, Jane Grigson (although how she ever came by a good chili recipe baffles me).

First make a sauce from hot and sweet red peppers (if you use dried chili peppers, you really need a large red sweet pepper for the liquid part of the sauce, although dried chilies should be soaked as well) along with an onion and garlic. You make this sauce simply by pulverizing these ingredients, most easily accomplished in a food processor. Then, as in most chili recipes, you brown some meat; pour off most of the fat; reserve the meat while you soften an onion; add more crushed and chopped garlic and perhaps another pepper or two; and cook everything (including the meat) in the sauce.

Cook over a low heat until the meat is done and perhaps quite a bit longer, so the sauce can thicken. Now begin to adjust the flavor, first with a generous amount of dried cumin. If the flavor is too sharp, you can sweeten with a little brown sugar or molasses. Tomatoes are not needed because of the pepper sauce, but if you are used to having tomatoes in your chili, you can add either tomato paste or canned tomatoes. Western style is without beans, but you can also add pinto beans or kidney beans at this point. I usually skip the tomatoes, but add the beans.

Although Mrs. Grigson has generally sound ideas about chili, someone has misled her into the belief that Americans habitually drink coffee with chili. Quite rightly, she suggests beer instead.

DILL

You probably think that this discussion of dill is going to wind up with a recipe for dill pickles. Sad to report, I have never achieved any dill pickles that are worth eating. Mine end up tasting too much of salt, no matter whose advice I follow. Furthermore, my brother has had the same experience, although he is a capable cook. Despite this major lack, I still find dill to be one of the most useful herbs in the garden. Dill goes into bread, salads, fish dishes, and soups. We buy excellent dill pickles.

Dill can be grown either for its seeds or for its leaves. I find that I have lots of uses for the leaves, few for the seeds (especially since I have given up on dill pickles, which are flavored with seeds). I am told that in earlier times, children were given dill seeds to chew in church to keep them awake through long sermons. I have not determined if this works or not, as sermons are much shorter nowadays. Perhaps I should chew some dill seeds during late-night televison, which puts me to sleep as readily as children were sent to slumber by a preacher's discourse.

The leaves, however, have a fresh flavor that enlivens any dish for which they do not have too much competition. For some reason, the commercially dried leaves are called "dillweed," as if the growers went out into the meadows or forests to find it. Dillweed is, of course, just the dried leaves of the same plants from which dill seeds are taken. If the dillweed designation made any sense, the herb sold as dill ought to be called "dillweedseed." Aside from the problems in nomenclature, it should be noted that dill leaves do not produce much flavor when dried. So you should grow your own dill to have fresh dill in the summer (and maybe to have in a pot in the

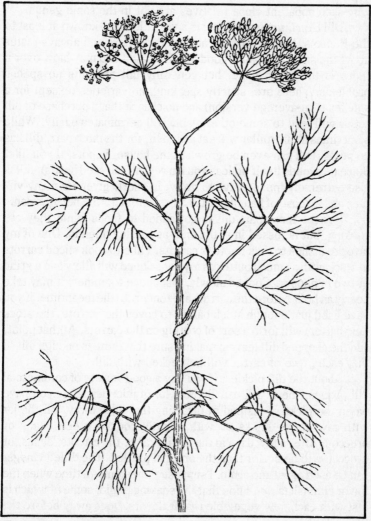

DILL (*Anethum graveolens*)

winter). It is sometimes possible to buy fresh dill leaves in markets, but you cannot count on it on any given day.

Dill looks a lot like fennel, although it is not so tall. If you grow both dill and fennel in the same garden, the seeds may not be any good from either, in any case. Dill and fennel are closely enough related to cross-fertilize. This does not affect the leaves of either, but it wrecks the seeds, both for flavor and for reproduction. Since dill and fennel produce nonreproducing hybrids, it is clear that they are in different species. But I am not enough of a botanist to know why such apparent close relatives are not in the same genus.

Dill (*Anethum graveolens*) is a very old herb, known at least to the Romans, that grows just about everywhere and always tastes about the same. It likes a good bit of sunlight and may blow over if there is too much wind, but generally dill presents no special problems. There are, strictly speaking, no varieties (except for a smaller-than-average version) and no chance that a purchase of dill seeds will lead to some other plant. Dill germinates easily. While sometimes a caterpillar will eat a bit of it, for the most part, dill has no pests. Dill can even be grown in the house, in pots, if you like. Since it reseeds itself (unless you harvest all the seed heads), dill is also extremely inexpensive to grow. In short, given its many virtues and its ease of handling, it is an essential for the herb garden.

For the most part dill is not added to foods while they are cooking, but is tossed in at the end, as parsley often is. One of my favorite dishes to toss it into is carrots. I like to cook sliced carrots in stock with as much butter as my conscience will allow and a grind or two of pepper. Cooked slowly, just above a simmer, it may take nearly an hour before the carrots are tender. In the meantime, if you have used just enough stock barely to cover the carrots, the stock (and butter) will form a sort of coating on the carrots. At that point, add the chopped dill leaves, making sure that there is enough dill so that each piece of carrot will be flecked with dill.

About the dill pickles: if you buy a good variety of commercial dill pickles, there will usually be a lot of juice left after you have eaten the pickles. Instead of throwing that juice away, fill the jar with raw carrot sticks or with slightly cooked green beans or broccoli. After a few days in the refrigerator, the carrots, beans, or broccoli will be better than the original pickles. The dilled vinegar can be used again and again. I suppose there comes a time when the flavor diminishes, but I find that the soaking liquid, some of which is lost with each new vegetable that it flavors, goes away before the flavor does.

EGYPTIAN ONIONS

A few years ago I found myself sharing a long automobile trip with a woman who was involved with both organic and herb gardening. She was having a problem with her garlic; it rotted instead of producing plants. She thought that perhaps the garlic she bought in supermarkets had been treated in some way to prevent it from sprouting. While I thought that unlikely (I have successfully grown garlic bought in supermarkets), I volunteered to give her some garlic I had grown, which I did. In response, she sent me a whole lot of bulbils from her Egyptian onions, along with instructions for planting. I heard later that the garlic I sent her had grown nicely. The Egyptian onions have been unstoppable.

Bulbils, by the way, are little bulblike growths that appear at the top of some members of the lily family. They are, except for their odd location, almost exactly like the fleshy bulbs that grow underground and produce tulips, daffodils, garlic, or onions. Because the apparent "fruit" of the plant is at the top instead of at the bottom, as in regular onions, Egyptian onions are sometimes called "top onions." Actually, the bulbs of Egyptian onions are quite small, like those of scallions.

The bulbils at the top are for reproductive purposes. I am continually amazed at the reproductive inventiveness of the lily family. The bulbs reproduce underground, causing two or more plants to spring up in the same small area. While this works fairly well for daffodils, succeeding generations of most lilies produced in this way become smaller, as the resources of the same small patch of ground are strained. So some lilies produce bulbils—not just top onions, either. Garlic, for example, will sometimes produce bulbils. As the stem bearing the bulbil bends over from the weight of the bulbil or from old age, the bulbil reaches the ground a foot or so away from the parent plant, where it can take root.

In this way, the lily can spread away from the immediate vicinity of the bulb. And, of course, lilies produce flowers and seed as well. Some lilies favor one of the three strategies over the others, but others—garlic being a prime example—will use all three as the occasion seems right. In my garden, at least, the Egyptian onion reproduces by multiplying the bulbs underground, since I harvest the bulbils and none of the onions have flowered.

Growing the Egyptian onion (*Allium cepa aggregatum*) is no problem. Once some bulbils have been planted, no care is needed that I can discern. The problem is figuring out what to do with them

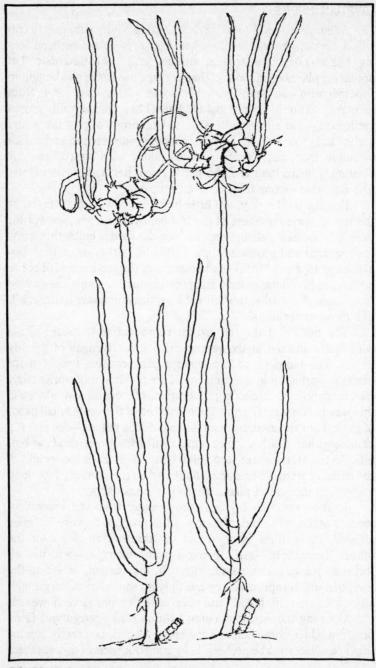

EGYPTIAN ONION *(Allium cepa aggregatum).*

124

after you have them growing. I looked in various books and received little help and what there was conflicting.

My first thought was to pull up an onion and use the bulb. There was not much bulb, and its flavor was strong and rather wild—somewhat like that of a wild leek. I did not repeat the experiment. Then I learned that the stems, when they are young, make good green onions—still stronger than scallions, but not so wild tasting as the bulbs. In the early spring, they are more available than chives and have more of an oniony flavor. I put them into Chinese-style stir-fries at the end, so that they are warmed but not cooked. Finally, I started using the bulbils in place of shallots. This was a happy idea, although the flavor is really not the same as shallots. A tablespoon of Egyptian onion, chopped fine, however, produces excellent results in making *bifsteak haché,* or French hamburger.

Make as many half-pound hamburgers as you have guests. Use a garlic press with garlic oozing out to finish shaping each burger, so it is liberally coated with garlic juice. Heat a large cast-iron skillet until a drop of water dances when you toss it into the skillet. Brown the burgers on both sides, then reduce the heat to cook them to the desired rareness. Add pepper and, if desired, salt. When the burgers are done, remove them to a warm platter and cover with foil. Pour out the fat. Add as much red wine as you need to cover the bottom of the skillet by about a quarter inch. Add an equal amount of stock. Place the skillet over a hot flame, and scrape the brown bits into the liquid as the liquid boils down. When about half the liquid is gone, put in a tablespoon or two of cornstarch that has been dissolved in port, sherry, vermouth, or stock. Reduce heat and stir until the sauce thickens. Correct seasoning and pour over each hamburger. Buns are optional.

If they are available, mushrooms can be cooked separately in butter or even in the fat from the hamburger (I add them while the hamburgers are still cooking, myself). The mushrooms, if cooked in hamburger fat, should be removed while the sauce is being made, then added to the sauce after it has thickened.

FENNEL

Although I managed to miss the several wars of our generation through a lucky timing of my birth, there is one battlefield that I imagine I know by its scent. Overpowering any of the unpleasant stenches of pregunpowder war, the smell of the battle of Marathon must have been licorice. This revelation came to me when I learned that *marathon* was the Greek word for fennel, and that the valley of

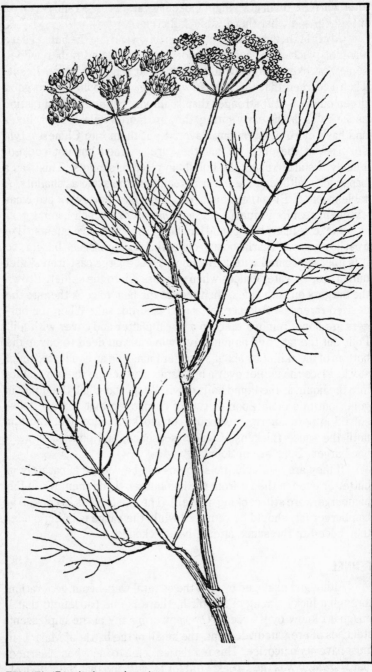

FENNEL (*Foeniculum vulgare*)

126

Marathon, where the famous battle was fought, was so called because of the abundant stands of fennel that grew there. Fennel smells exactly like, and tastes somewhat like, licorice. It is odd to think that the name for a race is derived from the name of a relative of the carrot.

Many herbs that are really quite different have this licorice association. Tarragon, chervil, and anise come readily to mind. Fennel is more like licorice than chervil or tarragon, but less like licorice than anise. Yet, in one of the principal uses of fennel seeds, there is no hint of licorice in the final product. Fennel seeds are an essential ingredient to many forms of Italian sausage, but their contribution is subtle, not overpowering at all.

The purest way to taste the flavor of fennel does not involve the herb at all. Fennel is also grown as a vegetable. Although the vegetable form is not a separate species, it is sufficiently different to be classed as a subspecies; thus, the herb is generally *Foeniculum vulgare*, while the vegetable is *Foeniculum vulgare dulce*. Some taxonomists, however, name the herb *Foeniculum officinale*.

This seems an appropriate point to comment on the meaning of some of these names. *Vulgare* is "common," so *F. vulgare*, as the botanists say, is "common fennel," while *F. vulgare dulce* is "sweet common fennel." *Officinale* means "medicinal," so *F. officinale*, or "medicinal fennel" recognizes that fennel is supposed to be good for what ails you. Many of the common herbs have *officinale* as part of their names—marsh mallow, bugloss, borage, calendula, fumitory, hyssop, jasmine, lovage, lemon balm, peppermint, watercress, rosemary, sage, wood betony, comfrey, dandelion, valerian, and speedwell appear on a list I just checked—which means that at the time they were given their scientific name it was believed that they had medicinal uses.

In some cases, these herbs are still used in either over-the-counter or prescription medicines. In other cases, books on herbs suggest their use as home remedies today. For most of us, however, the former medicinal herbs have become either flavorings or decorative plants.

To return to *F. vulgare*, fennel looks like a giant, or at least enlarged, version of its close relative, dill. Although potentially a perennial, it is almost always grown as an annual, planted early if you want the seeds for sausage. *F. vulgare dolce* is somewhat smaller but has large swellings at the base.

While the vegetable fennel, often called by its Italian name of finochio, can be cooked, finochio is usually served raw either before or toward the end of a true Italian feast. Its bright licorice flavor clears the palate for what follows or separates the meat course from the dessert. Raw finochio is also added to salads. If cooked, it is braised in stock.

The herb fennel may be used either for its leaves or its seeds. The leaves make an excellent addition to broiled or steamed fish. For an excellent low-calorie main course, coat firm-fleshed fish fillets, such as sole or flounder, with a spray of oil, and sprinkle with chopped fennel leaves, then broil on both sides or steam until the flesh flakes easily, about eight to ten minutes. With a fatter fish, such as bluefish, fennel not only adds to the flavor, but seems to cut the oiliness. Fennel seeds can be used to improve the flavor of a pork stew.

Sauté an onion and the brown pork cubes in olive oil or in rendered pork fat. (To render the fat, trim all the fat from the pork, cook the fat in a little water until the water evaporates, then fry the pieces of fat slowly until they are crisp. The crisped fat should be removed, but it can be added to other dishes for flavor, while the liquid fat remaining in the pan is the rendered fat.)

Add stock and some wine or calvados to cover the meat, along with a generous quantity of fennel seeds (about a teaspoon of seeds per pound of pork). Simmer until done, then degrease the sauce. Thicken by making a paste of flour and some of the sauce in a cup, then add the paste to the rest of the sauce and simmer until the sauce thickens and the flour cooks. (In fact, you may want to cook the paste for two or three minutes before adding it to the sauce, stirring constantly while the paste cooks.)

GARLIC

Nothing could be easier and more practical than growing garlic—at least if you favor European or Chinese cooking. I grow a lot of garlic, but I tend not to allot enough space to garlic some years, so I find that we have to buy garlic in the later winter in those years. Since garlic does not take up much space, and since we have *never* had too much garlic, this is just poor planning on my part.

Although by every reasonable criterion garlic is a herb, the place to grow it is in the vegetable garden. Also, although garlic is a perennial, there is no point to it unless you grow it as an annual. That means that you must plant it and harvest the whole plant each year, but nothing could be easier. My method is as follows: on a warm day in November I pick the spot in the vegetable garden that

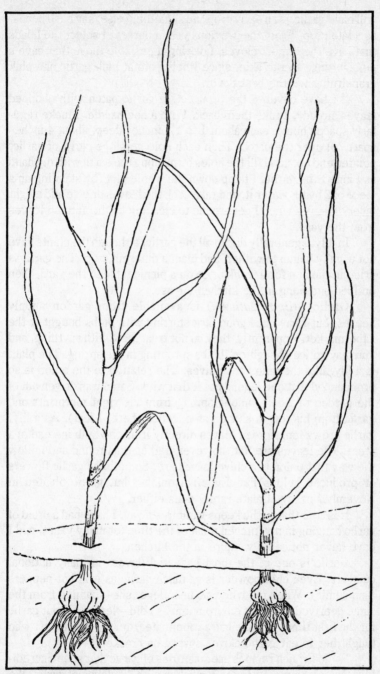

GARLIC (*Allium sativum*)

129

will have garlic as an early crop and something else, say bush beans, as a late crop. From the previous year's harvest I select the heads that have the largest cloves, favoring if possible those that have a pinkish tinge to the skin, since I believe that pink garlic and pink grapefruit have the best flavor.

If I have covered the prospective garlic patch with chopped leaves already, I rake them back. With a hoe handle, I make regularly spaced holes, each about 1 to 1½ inches deep, about 4 inches apart, all over the patch. Then each hole gets one clove of garlic, pointed end up, and I fill the holes by pushing the earth with my hand as I insert the garlic. I tamp down the whole plot (by standing on a piece of 2 by 8), water it, and rake back the leaves or else add a light layer of leaves when I get around to cleaning up the autumn leaves from the yard.

In July, I generally dig up all the garlic, although the plants have not usually begun to wither, and plant a different crop. The garlic is dried in the sun for a week or so on a picnic table in the yard, then braided and hung in the kitchen for use.

Garlic (*Allium sativum*) is available from garden supply houses, but I have had good luck starting with bulbs bought at the supermarket. Apparently, they do not treat them with anything, and you may notice "boughten" bulbs sprouting in the spring. The plant is a lily, like the onion and chives. The relation to the onion is so pronounced that one legend has it that when Satan was driven out of the garden of Eden, onions sprang from his right footprints and garlic from his left (a slur on an excellent herb, I fear). As a lily, garlic grows long, green leaves directly from the bulb instead of a stem. The leaves are flat, however, rather than round and hollow the way that onion and chive leaves are. Sometimes garlic flowers or produces bulbils like Egyptian onions, but garlic planted in November in my climate rarely does either.

It is true that garlic keeps vampires away. I have had a braid of garlic hanging in my kitchen most of the time for many years, and I have never noticed a vampire in the kitchen.

Garlic is one of the most essential flavors in many national cuisines. Even chili powder is as much garlic as it is hot peppers (and cumin). When my wife was in college, she—coming from the same deprived Midwest environment as I did—learned about garlic for the first time. But she had a roommate from the Southwest who taught her to eat garlic cloves spread on crackers!

Some French recipes use quantities of garlic that seem incredible. One of the most famous is chicken with 40 cloves of garlic. We mentioned this dish once to a garlic-loving friend who was staying in our house while we were away for the weekend. When we returned, she smelled so heavily of garlic that we were almost overpowered at the door. She had looked up the recipe, cooked it, eaten it for dinner, and was leaving a generous supply for us. The truth is, no matter how bad she smelled, the chicken was delicious, so I'll proffer the recipe here.

Usually for the notes on a specific herb I restrict myself to recipes that are an idea, with no exact measurements allowed, but in this case I have to break the rule. You *must* use exactly 40 cloves of garlic. They should be unpeeled. Put them and enough olive oil to cover the bottom of an ovenproof casserole in the casserole along with the chicken. Add a *bouquet garni*, and roll the chicken round in the oil so that it is covered on all sides. Seal the lid of the casserole with flour-and-water paste and bake in a moderate oven for about an hour and a half (more if you are a worrier). Unseal the casserole. Carve and serve the chicken with the garlic and browned croutons, good French bread, or crackers. The garlic should be squeezed from its skin onto the bread and eaten as an accompaniment to the chicken—along with a large quantity of dry white wine.

LEMON BALM

Lemon balm is not even mentioned in many books on flavoring, although it usually appears—frequently under its other name, melissa—in works devoted strictly to herbs. As far as I can recall, I have never seen this herb called for under either name in a general recipe book (or, for that matter, in a herb-oriented cookbook), although I have read—in a herb book—that lemon balm is used in veal and chicken dishes. The *New York Times* food writer Craig Claiborne once wrote a whole book on *Cooking with Herbs & Spices* in which he relegated lemon balm to a section entitled "Herbs and Spices with Limited, Quaint or Questionable Virtues."

In the section, he suggests that lemon balm could be used to flavor fruit cups, salads, fish dishes, or cream soups. If I wanted to use a lemony herb in veal or chicken dishes, or in fish dishes or cream soups, however, I would use lemon thyme so as to get the combination of lemon and thyme. Perhaps there is some role for lemon balm in fruit cups or salads, although I would think that straight lemon juice might work better. Nevertheless, lemon balm is a delightful and useful herb. I could live without it if I had to, but since I don't have to, I prefer to live with it.

Except—I wish I had contained the first plant I bought. While the extent of the problem varies from year to year, some years I have lemon balm appearing all over the herb garden. In degree of invasiveness, it is only behind peppermint; during the worst attacks, it is ahead of peppermint, both figuratively and literally. Although lemon balm (*Melissa officinalis*) is technically a perennial, it is not the kind that leaves a distinct plant above the ground all winter. In the following spring, however, the plant springs up in a slightly different place as well as several yards away—but it is the same plant. If you did not know what was happening, it would be easy to believe that the new plants were caused from seeds and that the original plant had simply died. Actually, some of the plants may *be* from seeds, since not only does lemon balm spread underground, but also it freely self-sows.

Lemon balm is not a showy plant, but neither is it unattractive. Some garden books think it should be kept in an out-of-the-way corner of the garden because it can be "weedy," but I have never noticed that trait. In overall appearance lemon balm is rather like a basil that has rougher, more serrated leaves than basil does. The small flowers, instead of being on a spike like those of basil, grow, mintlike, near the stem and on top of the leaves. A bed of lemon balm planted closely would have attractive green leaves all summer, as well as a pleasant scent when bruised, a scent that is exactly like that of a lemon. Although lemon verbena—a tropical plant that must be kept indoors all winter, where it does very poorly (in my house at least)—is highly touted as a lemon-flavored plant. I prefer lemon balm. Lemon verbena has a more powerful lemon scent, but I find something too assertive, almost rank, in the verbena. Lemon thyme is less lemony and has a thyme flavor and scent mingled with the lemon. For my money, lemon balm is the herb of choice for a pure lemon effect without the lemon.

I once had a persistent daydream in which I ran a restaurant that grew all its own food, so that the patrons could inspect the farm before they dined (in my daydream, this did not discourage the diners, as it might in real life with regard to the meat or poultry). It slowly dawned upon me that the dream was impossible, because I could not imagine cooking without lemons. But that was before I discovered lemon balm!

It should be mentioned that lemon balm does tend to lose some of its lemon scent and flavor if it is not dried immediately or carefully. This is not a problem with fresh balm, of course. I am told that if lemon balm is not dried within two days, it will turn black. Since I cannot imagine drying a herb other than immediately after

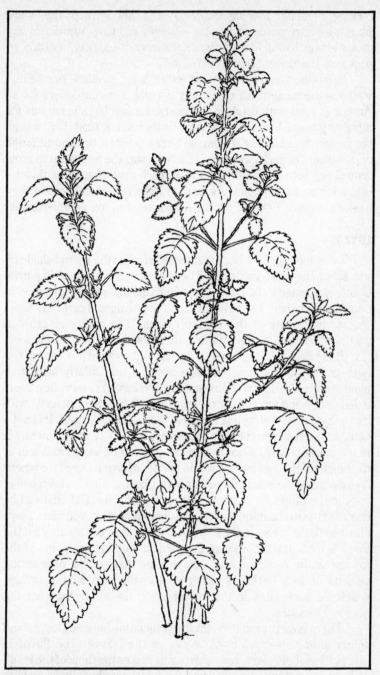

LEMON BALM (*Melissa officinalis*)

133

picking, I wonder how anyone discovered this. Perhaps they were planning to dry outdoors and the weather suddenly turned. In any case, lemon balm, like all herbs, is best dried fairly quickly to preserve the flavor, scent, and color.

Sometimes you will find that lemon balm is called "bee balm," which is the name most commonly used by herb gardeners for an American mint with bright red flowers. Lemon balm is famous for attracting bees. I would not know this if I had not read it. Although the genus name *Melissa* is from the Greek word for bee and although early writers of herbals claimed that balm was the best plant to grow around bee hives, bees do not spend much time around the flowers of my lemon balm plants. As near as I can tell, it is because they prefer oregano. Perhaps I have Italian bees in my neighborhood.

LOVAGE

I was looking for a herb that would grow in the partial shade on one side of my herb garden, and because lovage will grow in partial shade, it seemed to be the answer. Perhaps that is why lovage is so popular in England and in English cooking. England certainly lacks the sunny climate of the Mediterranean. The ability to grow in partial shade was certainly the main attraction of lovage for me.

It is just as well to have lovage tucked away in a corner of the herb garden in any case. Lovage is not a particularly attractive plant. Often it is described as looking like a giant celery; however, it has much longer and more separated stems than celery, with clusters of large, celerylike leaves at the top of each stem. It is not a neat, compact bunch the way that celery usually is when you buy it in the market. Also, since lovage can grow to be as tall as 5 feet at the height of the summer, it would not do to have it in a place where it could shade the other, more sun-loving herbs. Finally, lovage dies back in the fall to form an ungainly pile of dried stalks that can be unattractive in the middle of the garden. Of course, you can always clean up those stalks in the fall, but it is an unnecessary chore if the mess is back in the corner of the garden. Then the remains of the lovage can be removed at the same time that you do your spring cleanup of such herbs as tarragon, oregano, and winter savory, which die back later in the winter when no one cares what the garden looks like.

There is no reason to doubt the association between lovage and celery after you smell or taste one of the leaves. The flavor is distinctly that of celery, only sharper. It makes me think of the smell of my grandmother's turkey dressing, which was heavily laced with

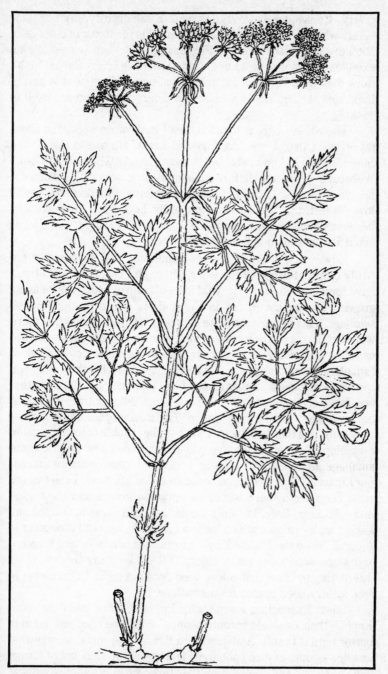

LOVAGE (*Levisticum officinale*)

celery. Consequently, lovage is quite a satisfactory substitute for celery when the main thing that is desired is the flavor of celery and not necessarily the crunch. For example, lovage leaves are an excellent addition to stock or to soups that have celery flavor. I don't think they would be useful in salads that have crunchiness as part of their appeal. The seeds also have a celery flavor and are used in cooking.

The name *lovage* is unusual, and I have often wondered about its origin. (Also, I wondered how to say it. No one in the United States seems to know whether to say "love-AAGE" or "LOVE-ij." Webster's gives the latter, inelegant as it sounds.) Like most people, I suppose, I thought that it must have something to do with love. In fact, that was an attraction of the herb when I first grew it, because people, on hearing that I was growing lovage, made jokes about its presumed aphrodisiac qualities.

However, I recently learned something that suggests an entirely different origin of the word, although I cannot be sure that I have found the answer. The wild form of celery, which can be found growing in suitable places in England, is called by the English *smallage*. This suggests that the English early recognized that there were two forms of a celery like plant, small and large. If the generic name for the celery plant was simply *age*, then one would speak of "small age" and "large age." If this theory is right, then smallage continues to have a similar name after centuries, but the form that was more commonly used in cooking acquired a contracted version of "large age" and became lovage *(Levisticum officinale))*.

With this theory in hand, I went to the trouble of looking up the etomologies in a dictionary, which confirmed my theory about smallage, but claimed that *lovage* is derived from *ligusticum*, meaning Ligurian. This makes no sense to me at all, since I can't figure what connection there would be between lovage and the region around Genoa, Italy. Possibly the dictionary makers have confused lovage with cardoon, which looks a bit like lovage and is popular in Liguria. Since the Middle English forms are smalache and lovache, and since ache does mean celery, I'll stick to my theory. (It is interesting to know that celery seed does not come from celery. In fact, celery seed comes from smallage.)

Since I associate lovage with England, what could be more English than Brussels sprouts soup? Cook some chopped onion in butter until it is soft. Add quartered Brussels sprouts, a somewhat smaller amount of diced potatoes, and a generous amount of lovage leaves. Cover and cook for another three or four minutes without browning the vegetables. Add enough stock to cover the vegetables by an inch or two, and simmer until the potatoes and Brussels sprouts are tender. Chop the whole mixture into a puree with a food processor, or put through the medium sieve of a food mill. Reheat. Just before serving, add a little cream and some more chopped lovage leaves.

MARJORAM

The authorities have currently decided that the scientific name for the common marjoram is *Majorana hortensis*, although older books use the Linnean name of *Origanum majorana*, marjoram oregano. It is easy to see why Linneaus was confused. Until it blooms, it is difficult to tell marjoram from either oregano or *Origanum dictamnus*, dittany of Crete. Another plant, similar to marjoram in flavor and appearance, is pot marjoram, *Majorana onites*, but pot marjoram does not have stems to its leaves. Often the whole group (except for dittany) is called *marjoram*, but with different adjectives: wild marjoram is oregano, pot marjoram is pot marjoram, and sweet marjoram is marjoram. Unless you want to know how hardy a plant is going to be, it probably doesn't matter that much, although oregano can be a lot stronger in flavor than marjoram. Marjoram is the least hardy (along with dittany), while oregano is the most hardy.

Because I have an unusually mild clump of oregano, I do not grow marjoram most years. On the other hand, even my mild oregano is too strong for, say, split-pea soup, in which I like to put a little marjoram. Since I eat split-pea soup mostly in the winter, dried marjoram is a staple. If you grow a few marjoram plants and dry them, then you are set up for soup for several years.

Another use I find for marjoram is in teas. Since I normally make herb teas from dried herbs, the same dried marjoram that is used as a flavoring suits just as well for tea. Actually, because the essential oil that gives marjoram much of its taste and fragrance is extremely volatile (although not quite so volatile as that of basil, or it would not survive drying), marjoram contributes more to the aroma of tea than to its taste.

Because marjoram is tidier than oregano, it can be used to better effect visually. Although its flowers are quite small, the foliage is generally grayer than that of oregano, a desirable trait in a herb garden. If it were hardier and could be grown up north like the perennial it is, marjoram would be an excellent component in a

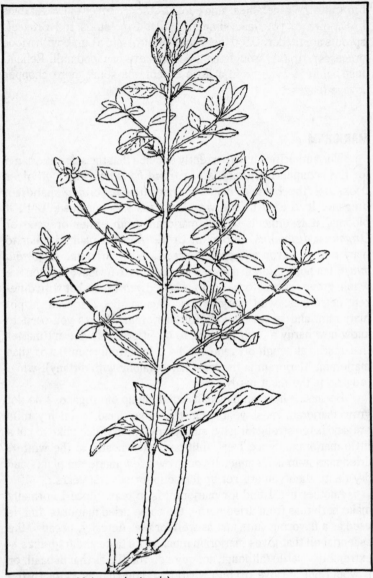

MARJORAM (*Majorana hortensis*)

formal herb garden. In fact, in milder climates, marjoram is used in this way. Where I live, marjoram needs to be replanted each year, which discourages such a use. More commonly, it is used as a grayish border that contrasts with the bright green of a flower garden.

I often substitute marjoram for thyme in a recipe, just for a change. While I would be unlikely to use marjoram in a dish that is clearly associated with thyme flavor, such as clam chowder, it seems to work well almost everywhere that thyme does. The two herbs can be used together to good effect as well. In fact, marjoram is a member of the mint family, as is thyme, and most of the milder mints seem to work well together (for example, oregano, basil, and rosemary, all mints, in Italian dishes). The stronger mints, such as mint itself or lemon balm, tend to overpower the others, so they do not fit as well into mixed herb flavorings.

Pea soup can mean many different things, but to me it means *potage St. Germaine*, French split-pea soup flavored with carrots, onions, and ham. I have never seen a recipe for *potage St. Germaine* that also uses marjoram, but it helps a lot, especially if you omit salt, as I generally do. Also, I eat more pea soup than I do ham, so my *potage* often fails to contain a ham bone. In that case, marjoram can become a principal flavor, instead of a bit player. The result—especially with fresh marjoram—is a delicately perfumed variation of the traditional *potage St. Germaine*.

Start by covering a package of split peas with water. Bring the water to a boil, then turn off the heat. Let the peas soak in the hot water for at least an hour.

Meanwhile, cook some sliced onions and chunked carrots in butter or, better yet, bacon fat. While they are cooking, add several grinds of black pepper. When the onions are soft and translucent, and all the onion rings have separated, add stock and the peas. You need a lot of stock, about a quart and a half, for the standard pound package of peas—and you may want to add more. Bring to the boil, then reduce to a simmer for a couple of hours, until the peas are tender. (If you have a ham bone, by all means simmer it along with the peas.) When the peas are done, chop the soup for a few seconds in a food processor or put through the medium disk of a food mill. Return to the fire and reheat with a half cup or a cup of milk or cream. Croutons from homemade bread can be added to the soup.

HEAD MINT

Everyone warns about mint escaping from confinement and taking over your garden. Indeed, mints are among the Willie Suttons of the plant world. Undeterred by the thought of a mass march of mints, I decided that two old automobile tires buried to be level with the soil would hold my spearmint and peppermint. Helpful hint: don't try it. After a couple of years of trying to get all the mint growing around the tires to retire, so to speak, I gave up on the project. The only thing that saved the entire garden was a paved rock area a few inches away from the tires. Although the rock very much slowed down the menacing advance, peppermint continues to spring up in cracks between the rocks and must be further discouraged each spring.

Peppermint normally refuses to spring up in the same place twice, which accounts for some of its traveling habits. Apparently, its underground roots travel away from home like exogamous Indians in the Amazon. However, given no escape—the peppermint will overcome its prejudice about growing twice in the same spot.

The truth is that, while peppermint is the worst spreader I have ever encountered, all perennial members of the mint family need to be confined. This includes many plants that you may not think of as mints, such as lemon balm and oregano. A practical solution for the herb garden may be tiles. A piece of tile at least 1 foot long (and preferably 1½ feet long) will do the job nicely. Just dig a hole as deep as the tile is long and plant the herb in the center of the tile—which should be about 6 to 8 inches from the rim of the tile.

In a short time, the herb will form a neat circular patch that will travel no farther. Such a patch is also easier to protect for the winter than the usual sprawl. The important thing to remember is to start with the herb in the tile. Don't make the mistake of trying to contain it after it has started to spread.

As mentioned above, I grow more peppermint *(Mentha piperita officinalis)* than I want and not enough spearmint *(Mentha spicata)*. I tried growing another mint, pennyroyal *(Mentha pulegium)*, because it was strongly suggested in a book about gardening that I liked. What the author failed to tell me was that pennyroyal has a very peculiar flavor, probably suited only to those who have grown up using it, and that this is the only mint that is not hardy as far north as New York State. I lost all my pennyroyal the first winter and I found that I did not miss it very much. The fourth type of mint is apple mint *(Mentha rotundiflia)*, which has a pleasant flavor, but hairy leaves. Certainly if you wanted to have one mint for mint julips and possibly for lamb, the one you would want is spearmint. If it is not competing with peppermint, spearmint is aggressive enough for any gardener.

The British do a lot with mint, but then the British do a lot of peculiar things with food. Mint is too strong for most foods. As suggested above, even lamb with mint sauce turns me off; I like lamb plain with a very good Bourdeaux. Aside from the mint julip,

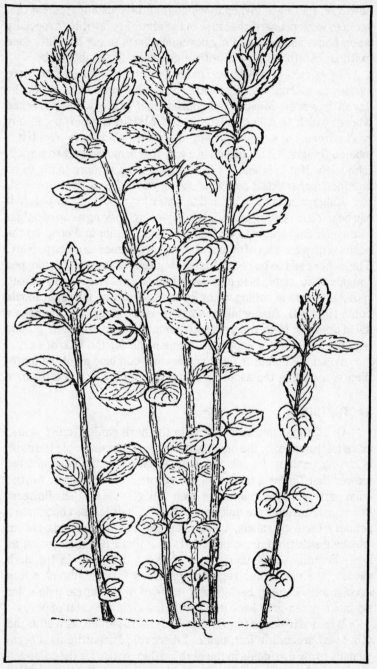

PEPPERMINT (*Mentha piperita*)

however, there are dishes in which mint is a main ingredient that seem to work primarily because of the mint. My favorite, especially when I am making one of my periodic efforts to eat healthier food (with an eye to losing a bit of weight as well) is tabbouleh.

Tabbouleh is a Middle-Eastern dish that actually has more parsley in it than any other herb. The mint provides most of the flavor, however. Most of the nourishment is provided by cracked wheat, which is called bulgur in the Middle East. You can buy cracked wheat or bulgur in health-food stores if nowhere else. If it is labeled "bulgur," it is cracked in a way that is more likely to work in tabbouleh. If it is labeled "cracked wheat," it is more likely to be intended for breakfast cereal, and it may even be partly precooked.

Bulgur needs to be soaked in water for about an hour before it can be used in making a salad. While you are soaking a cup of bulgur in enough cold water to cover it, you can gather and chop up the herbs. You want a lot of mint and about three times as much parsley. The mint needs to be chopped fine, but the parsley can be chopped roughly. You should also chop an onion, and peel and chop a tomato (put the tomato in boiling water for ten seconds, and the skin should come right off). Also while the bulgur is soaking, you can make a salad dressing from wine vinegar, lemon juice, and freshly ground pepper. Use a lot of pepper to compensate for the lack of salt.

When the bulgur is finished soaking, combine all of the ingredients, including the salad dressing. Serve on a bed of lettuce.

NASTURTIUM

Of all the plants that I grow in the herb garden (most years, since it is an annual), the one that seems to surprise people the most is the nasturtium. I think that it is assumed by the uninquisitive viewer that I grow a flower for the color, since herbs are, for the most part, more interesting for their foliage than for their flowers. In fact, nasturtiums are quite good to eat. Their leaves contribute a peppery taste to salads, while their pickled flower buds are an adequate substitute for capers. It is true that I like their looks, as well. For one thing, unlike most flowers that grow in the herb garden, the nasturtium regularly provides various vibrant colors against a dark green background, instead of the single pale color against a green-gray backdrop that is the common habit of herbs.

It is nice to have a few flowers in the herb garden, as well as the other way around. In fact, before I discovered nasturtiums, I occasionally grew marigolds in the herb garden, partly for the color and partly for the ability of marigold to repel some soil pests called nematodes. Nematodes do not seem to be a serious problem with herbs, however, so put your marigolds in the vegetable garden, where they will do more good. Bee balm (also called monarda, bergamot, and Oswego tea) has also contributed to the color of the herb garden in some years, but lately I have dug it up and donated it to my wife's perennial border. Bee balm is too tall for the herb garden, although the flowers are certainly showy. Also, it looks

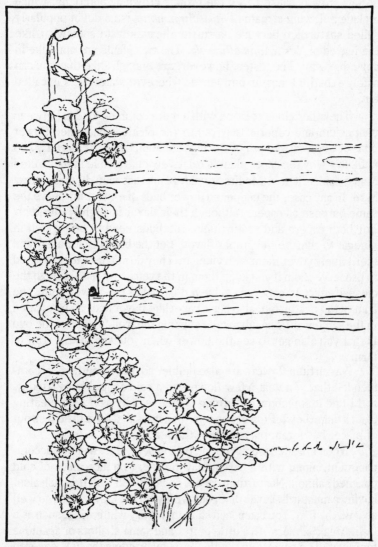

NASTURTIUM (*Tropaeolum majus*)

143

ghastly after it has finished flowering, so one needs to cut it down just at the time of year that everything else is going on. The bush-type nasturtium is really the best choice for color, fitting in nicely with the other herbs and providing a bonus in flavor.

Nasturtium (*Trapaeolum majus*) is one of those flowers, like geranium, for which the popular name and scientific name do not match. *Nasturtium officinale* is watercress, an excellent herb that I do not grow because I lack the proper growing conditions, which include a flowing stream. *Trapaeolum majus* is no doubt popularly called nasturtium because nasturtium leaves taste somewhat like the leaves of *Nasturtium officinale*. The two plants are not alike in any other way. The tastes, however, are enough alike that you can safely substitute nasturtium leaves wherever watercress is called for.

The other close relation with a more common food is between nasturtium and capers. Capers are the pickled, unopened flower buds of *Capparis spinosa* or the less common *Capparis inermis*. I do not know why the caper plant is relatively unavailable in the United States, since it is a Mediterranean plant that would surely grow here. In any case, the unopened flower buds of nasturtium serve the same purpose as capers, although their flavor is slightly different. For both capers and nasturtiums, the buds need to be pickled in vinegar to achieve the proper flavor. Let the buds dry for a day and then simply cover them with vinegar. They do not need to be cooked to preserve them if you keep them in the refrigerator. Although the closest effect to capers is achieved by using the flower buds, the fruit of the nasturtium also has a caperlike flavor and can be pickled in the same way. The advantage of using the fruit instead of the bud is that you also get to see the flower when you wait for the fruit to form.

Nasturtium flowers are also edible, so it is sometimes recommended that you float a few flowers in a cold soup. I have tried it, and I find it somehow disturbing. I feel vaguely as if I were eating from a fingerbowl. Flowers as a garnish in a salad are a little less out of place, but I generally stick to the leaves.

When I first encountered the true capers, they were an accompaniment, along with a herbal mayonnaise, to a nice piece of cold poached salmon. Nasturtium capers do very well with this dish also, having a mustardy flavor that goes well with the mayonnaise as well as with the fish. You can poach salmon in a dry white wine, such as a California chablis, with a little butter and some shallots or scallions for flavor. The easiest way to do this is by bringing the fish, covered with wine or a mixture of wine and water or fish stock, to a simmer on top of the stove, then put the poaching dish into a preheated oven for about ten minutes, or until the fresh flakes easily. Then cool and refrigerate, saving the liquid for another fish dish. When the salmon is cool, but not really cold, serve it with herbal mayonnaise and drained nasturtium capers (and a nice glass of real French chablis).

OREGANO

It is hard to believe that oregano was an unfamiliar flavor only a few years ago in the United States. There can be no doubt, however, that oregano was almost unknown here until after World War II. Before that time, for example, there is no record in the U. S. Customs that oregano had ever been imported. The flavoring is not mentioned in cookbooks until after the war, either. Certainly, Italian or Greek families may have somehow grown oregano, but the word of this excellent herb did not spread to the general public until American G.I.'s in Southern Italy discovered pizza *en masse*. Since there is no point to pizza without oregano, the herb began to be both imported and grown regularly. Perhaps its recent advent in this country accounts for some of the confusion about it.

Botanists seem to recognize only one species of oregano that is used for cooking, *Origanum vulgare*. Even they do not seem to be sure, however, of really good ways to differentiate oregano from marjoram. At least, the founder of classification, Linnaeus, seemed to think that they were nearly the same. He put them in the same genus.

Even the apparent differences of the plants are not always really different. For example, although it is true that oregano is generally raised as a perennial and marjoram as an annual, marjoram is perennial also if the climate and treatment suit it. Or is it that some varieties of marjoram are annual, others biennial, and others perennial?

Recently the botanists have decided that oregano and marjoram are unrelated at the genus level, which is a far cry from being different species within the same genus. Even so, it is not that easy to tell one from another. This variable family also poses identification problems for gardeners, as well as for botanists. When you buy an oregano plant in a store, you may get almost any flavor of plant, for example.

One school of thought holds that the difference in various types of oregano stem from differences in climate or soil. They claim, for instance, that the flavor of oregano grown in Southern Italy is more

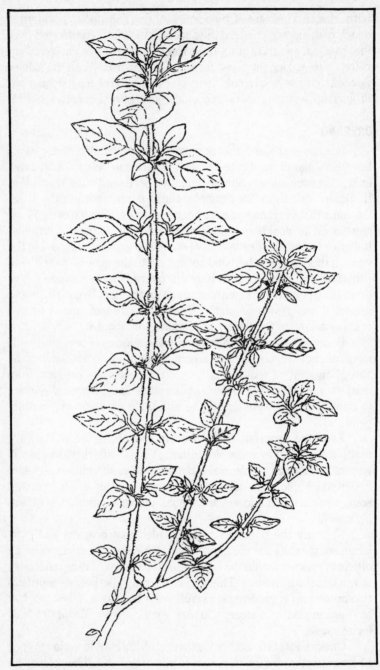

OREGANO (*Origanum vulgare*)

pungent than that of oregano grown in Northern Italy. There is probably something to this idea. Dried oregano that is sold in the United States was usually grown in sunny Mexico. It is definitely stronger in flavor than the oregano from my herb garden, even when my oregano is dried. Mexican oregano is akin in flavor to, but not quite the same as, imported dried oregano, which is typically grown in sunny Greece. But while Mexico and Greece are both sunny, no one would say that the climate or soil are the same in the two countries. Some authorities confuse the issue even further by saying that some Mexican oregano is really from an unrelated New World plant and that the Greek variety is actually another species of oregano.

Whatever! I strongly recommend oregano in the herb garden. Even if it turns out to taste more like marjoram than pizza, it is an excellent addition to all tomato sauces and contributes to many other dishes as well. Furthermore, if it is properly contained so that it does not spread, it is among the easiest and most trustworthy of herbs to grow.

I suppose that the appropriate thing to do at this point would be to supply a recipe for pizza. Pizza, however, is more complex than the simple recipes that go with the notes on individual herbs, so a pizza recipe is relegated to the section that follows. Instead I will tell you a little bit about baked eggplant.

We tend to grow more eggplant than any reasonable person would, so it is nice to have various ways to prepare it. Just baked plain and served hot is quite good, especially when we are dieting. But baked and served with oregano is better. Slice the eggplant lengthwise into ½-inch slices. Dip each slice in a pie pan that has a bit of olive oil in it, so that both sides of the slice are coated. Put the eggplant in a pan and bake in a hot oven for about ten minutes, one layer at a time. (You may want more than a single panful.) While it is still hot, drizzle some lemon juice and add a large quantity of chopped fresh oregano and a bit of ground pepper. Turn the eggplant slices to get lemon, oregano, and pepper on each side.

There is nothing wrong with eating this hot as a vegetable side dish, but the Italians, who invented it, serve it at room temperature. If you make a lot at one time, it will keep and improve in flavor in the refrigerator for two or three days. It can then be eaten either heated or simply warmed to room temperature.

PARSLEY

People who just eat and don't cook may recognize parsley as a

147

spritely sprig of unknown purpose that often appears as decoration on plates in pricey restaurants, or they may recognize it as the little specks of green that sometimes appear on otherwise unsullied boiled potatoes. On the other hand, cooks are more familiar with parsley as the herb that seems to go into almost every vegetable or meat dish at some stage in the preparation. The mild flavor of parsley is so ubiquitous in French-style cooking that you only miss the taste if it is not there—and then you may not miss it very much.

Parsley is the one herb that seems to be common in supermarkets all over the United States, so you really don't have to grow your own. On the other hand, why spend the same amount of money that it costs to buy a seed packet and just get some tired greens. The seeds will provide you with more parsley than you need year around.

Parsley can be harvested all year around both because it grows comfortably in a pot indoors and because of its growing habits. Parsley is strictly a biennial, like its close relative, the carrot. The first year you plant parsley, you get nothing but lovely leaves and stems. If you protect the plants for the winter, those same leaves and stems stay fresh under the snow. After the parsley has been uncovered in the spring, it begins to grow again. Soon a seed stalk emerges, bearing a type of flower called an umbel. After the flowers go and seeds form, the parsley has had it. The next winter the parsley will probably die, having fulfilled its destiny.

It must be noted that second-year parsley has a somewhat stronger flavor than first-year parsley and that the leaves are generally somewhat coarser. If you let the second-year parsley go to seed each year, however, you will find that the plant reseeds. The seeds germinate so slowly that, especially if they get into your compost, you will find parsley sprouts in the weirdest places around your garden ever after. (One word of caution: wild parsley, which has much more finely cut leaves than the domestic variety, is poisonous.)

Most books on herbs tend to make a big thing out of the difference between curly French parsley (*Petroselinum crispum*) and flat-leaved Italian parsley (*Petroselinum filcinum*), but I usually grow both. The flavor difference is not great, but Italian parsley is more prolific and French parsley is prettier.

If I have depleted much of my regular parsley supply it probably has been the result of preparing tabbouleh, a salad that is actually more parsley than it is anything else. You'll find a recipe for tabbouleh in the mint entry, however, as the flavor of mint tends to overpower the flavor of parsley. In fact, everything tends to over-power the flavor of parsley, just as parsley seems to contribute to the flavor of almost anything.

Here is a marvelous dish in which the flavor of parsley is dominated by the garlic, but which absolutely requires the parsley to come off right. The French call it *poulet persillade*, but I think of it

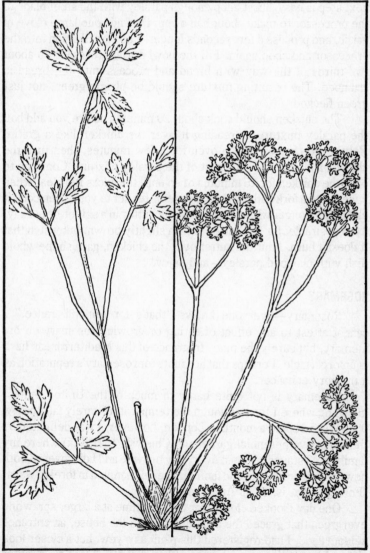

PARSLEY (*Petroselinum*) Italian (P. filcinum) left and French (P. eripsum) right.

as chicken with parsley. While you preheat the oven to 450°F, cut up a medium-size chicken into parts. Put enough good cooking oil to cover the bottom of a large cast-iron skillet or enameled casserole. Sprinkle the chicken pieces with some grinds of black pepper, and roll the pieces around in the skillet until they are coated with the oil. Heat the skillet on the stove. When it is hot enough that the chicken sizzles, put the skillet in the oven. If you have a food processor, the next step is easy. First chop enough parsley with the steel blade of the processor to make about half a cup, then add one large clove of garlic, and process a few seconds longer. Put a small onion into the processor and chop again. Fill the bowl of the processor up about two-thirds of the way with bread and process until the bread is crumbed. The resulting mixture should be plainly green, not just green flecked.

The chicken should cook about 20 minutes before you add half the parsley mixture, spreading it over the chicken like a gratin. Return the chicken to the oven for a few minutes, then turn the chicken and spread on the rest of the parsley mixture. Continue to bake the chicken for 15 minutes or so until the juices run clear when poked with a fork and the chicken seems tender to you. Then cook it just a little longer while you melt some butter in a skillet. It is okay, even desirable, for the butter to turn slightly brown, but watch that it doesn't burn. Pour the butter over the chicken, garnish the whole dish with chopped parsley—and enjoy.

ROSEMARY

Rosemary—everyone knows "that's for rememberance." I cannot attest to any effect of eating or growing rosemary on my memory, but surely the piney fragrance of this Mediterranean herb is unforgettable. Perhaps that accounts for rosemary's reputation as a memory enhancer.

Rosemary is not quite hardy in much of the United States, including where I live, although the temperature rarely falls below 0°F. When I spent a month in London, however, I was delighted by the extensive perennial gardens in Chiswick (CHIS-ik) where my family and I stayed. Almost every day my wife and I discovered both new and exotic flowers and familiar species handled in foreign ways. (Foreign, that is, to an American.)

One day I looked closely for the first time at a large, sprawling evergreen that graced the front entrance to the house, an entrance seldom used. I had registered this plant as a yew, but a closer look showed me that I was mistaken. Although it was 3 feet in diameter

150

ROSEMARY (*Rosemarinus officinalis*)

and at least as tall, the "yew" was to all appearances a giant rosemary plant. Breaking off the tip of one of the branches brought firm conformation from my nose. So even if I have to move both my rosemarys into the house each fall, I know that they would thrive outdoors all year in a climate as mild as London's, at least in a sheltered spot. In fact, since then I have learned of a Medieval legend that suggests the natural size of rosemary when conditions are perfect for growth.

Rosemary, we are told, felt that out of respect for the Lord it should never grow any taller than Jesus had been when He walked the earth. Therefore, it will grow only to the height of an ordinary man; thereafter, it simply spreads.

Where winters are cold, however, it would be difficult to grow a rosemary plant taller than about 2 feet. No matter. Rosemary makes a striking houseplant. If you have a sunny spot in the house and can refrain from either overwatering or underwatering, you can keep a healthy plant in a pot close to the size of the roots. Although it is a bit more trouble, a potted rosemary grows even better with a summer outdoors in the herb garden and a visit in the house during the winter.

There are two basic forms of rosemary, erect and lazy. The lazy, or prostrate, rosemary (*Rosemarinus prostratus*) makes the more striking houseplant for two reasons. As it grows, the lower branches dip lower and lower, trailing down until they will hang below a pot that is suspended. Also, in the fall, winter, or early spring, prostrate rosemary that has had full sun all summer is likely to reward you with tiny blue-lavender flowers scattered profusely along its branches. While the more common upright form (*Rosemarinus officinalis*) also flowers occasionally, the flowers are much rarer. Indeed, I have never seen them. I had the thought that if we could have stayed in London a few more months, we might have seen the giant rosemary by the front door covered with blue flowers at Christmas, a nice change from poinsettia. The books tell me, however, that upright rosemary is more likely to flower in the spring.

Although the common upright form is bashful about flowering, it has the better cooking qualities. The flavor is better and there are more soft growing tips. The woody growth of the prostrate rosemary often penetrates to the end of the branch, making it necessary to strip the leaves from the twig before using them. Since the leaves of this form are sharp little spikes, less than half an inch long, this operation can be an unpleasant complication. You can, however, snip the growing tips of the stand-up rosemary and chop or snip the whole tip to bits with no difficulty. Furthermore, the gray-green leaves of the upright rosemary are both longer and softer than the tiny darts of the prostrate form.

In fact, for my favorite dish with rosemary, roast pork, you do not even have to chop. For a 3 to 5-pound loin of pork, simply snip a half-dozen or so tips from the plant. Make slits about an inch deep at scattered locations around the roast. Use the tip of your knife to wedge a rosemary tip in each slit. Also, in another scattered group of a half-dozen slits, insert—with your fingers this time—a whole, peeled clove of garlic. In summer, I roast the pork on a charcoal grill equipped with a rotisserie, but the loin tastes almost as heady and wild when roasted on a rack in a pan in a preheated 350°F oven for a couple of hours. Timing is less important than internal temperature. A meat thermometer should register 180°F.

SAGE

Of all the perennial herbs in my garden, the day-to-day future of sage has concerned me the most. Perhaps my problems stem from an old folk saying, which may be an old folk truth. Sage does well when its owner is thriving, but droops when he or she is in financial difficulty. Since I am from time to time in considerable financial difficulty, my sage has from time to time dropped into the ground. Sometimes it has had to be replaced by new plants (although I have never quite gone bankrupt). In any case, my sage has mysteriously failed when I could discern no particular reason for the failure. I wish you better fortune, both with your sage and your finances.

Nevertheless, I maintain my sage crop by keeping more plants than I do the more trustworthy winter savory or oregano, which supply more leaves than I need. So does sage, but I hate to think that the day I am planning saltimbacca for dinner, I will go out and find that my single sage plant has decided it is time to fold up its tent. While all the sage plants seem to go through spells at once, I can count on one or two of the four or five plants to resist somewhat the megrims. I always have sage when needed.

Lately, I have taken to varicolored sages, plants that may have reddish leaves with green borders, or leaves that are quite golden. These do as well as the gray-green perennial I was wont to grow on the grounds that ornamental varieties could not have good flavor. In fact, the ornamental sages so far seem to have exactly the same flavor as the common garden variety.

Sage (*Salvia officinalis*) is a close relative of the salvia with the bright red flowers that is a common element in many flower gardens. While the flowers of sage are not so showy, the small sage blossoms are the same shape and in the same arrangement as the large red flowers of salvia. Sages should not be confused with sagebrush, an entirely different plant that gets part of its name from a resemblance in the scent of sagebrush to that of sage.

SAGE (*Salvia officinalis*)

There is another species of sage that is often grown in herb gardens, pineapple sage (*Salvia rutilans*). It shares the bright red blossoms with salvia but is not quite dramatic enough to be a good garden flower. (It does make a nice houseplant.) Pineapple sage is not very useful in cooking, as the pineapple scent of its leaves does not transmit to the dish nor does much of any other flavor. Furthermore, although pineapple sage is a perennial, it is not hardy at all. If it is grown north of Florida, it needs to be grown in a pot and brought indoors before the first hint of a frost.

Ordinary sage is quite hardy if given a light mulch in the winter.

The leaves that stay green into the late fall with such a mulch can be harvested fresh for the stuffing for the Thanksgiving turkey—and possibly for the Christmas turkey as well.

In the United States, the main use for sage is in stuffing. It goes well with turkey and goose, but is perhaps not the best way to stuff a chicken or duck. Italians have found many other uses for sage, particularly in veal dishes, but most Americans or Britons use it strictly for stuffing. In the tradition of the country, I will provide my recipe for sage stuffing.

First make some bread. Failing to make your own bread, try to buy some French or Italian bread that was made without sugar or other additives. The same large bowl in which your bread has risen (or another large bowl) should be filled to the top with crumbs of bread, pinched out with your fingers. Then toast the crumbs in the oven until they are a light brown. Now toss the toasted crumbs in the bowl with sage and pepper. Pour a quantity of melted butter on the crumbs, and toss again. Sauté a couple of chopped onions with finely diced celery and add to the bread crumbs. Toss. Pour a fairly large amount of grated swiss cheese on the crumb mixture, and toss again.

Beat a couple of eggs, with some cream added if you like. Add the eggs to the crumb mixture, and toss once more. Ideally you should have enough dressing (as we call it in the Middle West) to stuff both cavities of the bird and also to fill an ovenproof dish. The dish should be put in the oven about an hour before the bird is done. With a bulb baster, every ten minutes or so—while you also baste the bird—you should drizzle about half a cup of liquid from the roasting pan over the stuffing in the bowl. When all is finished, you won't know whether to prefer the stuffing in the bowl or the stuffing in the bird, although both will be good.

Both will be better, by the way, if you add either as many braised chestnuts as you care to peel or as many small link sausages as your conscience will permit before stuffing the bird or filling the bowl.

TARRAGON

Today I find it hard to believe that I had never heard of tarragon until I was in my thirties. A friend who had married into a French family first mentioned it to me. She had obtained a cutting of tarragon from another gardener, but her plant had no flavor, although the mother plant had the true tarragon taste (a combination of licorice and vanilla that is more subtle than either). She suspected that the daughter plant did not get enough sun in her garden. Somehow this conversation stuck in my mind, so when I bought my own tarragon plant at a local nursery some years later, I made sure that it had the sunniest spot in the herb garden.

Growing up in the midwestern United States, neither my wife nor I had ever encountered the flavor of tarragon. When I began to learn French cooking, I was surprised to find tarragon occurring over and over in recipes. That's when I bought my plant. At first, I was a bit afraid of it, since the unfamiliar taste seemed to overpower dishes. Soon, however, I came to relish it so much that I even like salads that have a handful of fresh tarragon leaves tossed along with the other greens. My wife has never quite got used to it to this day, however, unless it is used sparingly. It has long been recognized as a healthful substitute for salt, so I am trying to get her more interested in its flavor.

I have read a lot of advice about how to grow tarragon, and all of it is different. My tarragon gets some straw mulch in the winter, but it always dies back to the ground level anyway. However, since tarragon normally propagates from rhizomes (a rhizome is a form of stem that grows underground, which the casual observer would think is a root), it comes to life every spring. Usually, the rhizomes that put forth the new shoots are a few inches away from where the plant that grew last year had been. Therefore, I have to adjust my permanent rock mulch slightly each time. More than one plant emerges each spring, which is why it is necessary to divide tarragon every three or four years. There is some reason to believe that this cycle of death and transfiguration is necessary to tarragon. I have heard that tarragon cannot be grown reliably in regions where the ground does not freeze.

French tarragon *(Artemisia dracunclus)* seems to be associated with dragons for reasons that I have not been able to determine. The French name, *estragon,* and the species name both refer to dragons. The English word is identified as derived from Arabic, although it is hard to see how Arabs could grow tarragon on their climate. (The conventional theory is that tarragon originated somewhere in central Russia, although it is not noticeable as a flavoring in any of the traditional Russian dishes.) Some books say that the taproot of the tarragon plant reminded people of a dragon's tail, but I say that is like believing that the Big Dipper looks like a bear.

Lists of what types of food benefits most from each herb are generally inconsistent. I was surprised recently to come across one

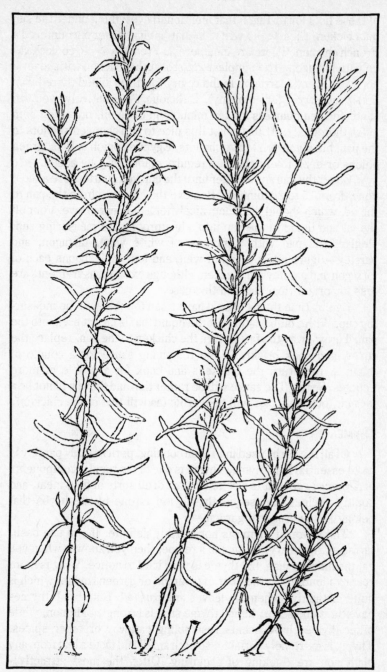

TARRAGON (*Artemisia dracunculus*)

of those lists for tarragon that mentioned everything under the sun but chicken. Clearly the writer of that list had never encountered a French chicken. There are innumerable French ways to cook chicken with tarragon. The simplest is to roast the chicken with several sprigs of French tarragon in the cavity (perhaps joined there by an onion and carrot for company). Delicious. Alternatively, you can sauté chicken quarters for ten minutes in olive oil, browning both sides thoroughly. At that point it is nice to add chopped shallots to the pan, but if you don't have shallots, Egyptian onion bulbils, green onions or even finely chopped regular onions may be added.

Cover the pan and simmer until the chicken quarters are almost done, from 15 to 20 minutes. Remove the chickens from the pan to the lid, which should hold them nicely for a moment or two. Pour off the fat and liquid in the pan into a heatproof glass measuring cup. Deglaze the pan with a mixture of white wine, tarragon, and parsley—figure about a cup of wine and four tablespoons each of tarragon and parsley per chicken, although exact measurements are less important than usual in this case.

By this time the fat should have risen to the top of the measuring cup. With a bulb baster, put the liquid that is not fat back into the pan. Throw away the fat. Return the chicken to the pan, replace the cover, and cook briskly in the remaining sauce for a couple of minutes, then turn the chickens and cook for a couple of more minutes. Serve. The sauce will be rather thin and there will not be a lot of it, but the flavor will be terrific (as will that of the chicken).

THYME

Of all the herbs used in French cooking, perhaps only parsley is more essential than thyme. Thyme is one of the regular components of a *bouquet garni*. It is a common part of all sorts of fish, meat, and poultry recipes. Consequently, thyme is one of the herbs that belong in any practical garden.

The flavor of thyme is not terribly definite. If you use basil, tarragon, rosemary, or sage in a recipe, then you know it when you eat the finished dish, but thyme is very hard to notice. What is more readily identified is the oder of common or garden thyme, which is quite distinctive when the leaves are crushed. But not all thymes have the same scent; lemon thyme smells strongly of lemon, while other thymes have scents resembling caraway or other spices. Thyme is extremely variable, so both smell and taste a leaf from any plant you are thinking of acquiring. Often the most attractive-looking plants have a bitter flavor, while the least attractive ones are likely to have the richest and most rewarding taste. You cannot go by scent alone, as the acrid quality of thyme, desirable in small amounts, may be too great for cooking, and the bitterness does not show up in the odor.

Thyme comes in all sorts of sizes and shapes (although none of the plants are very big). Not only are several related species called thyme, but within one of the species there can be considerable variation. Each new thyme plant I have bought has looked different from the others. (I am referring to common or garden thyme *Thymus vulgaris*, the plant that is most commonly used in cooking.)

I also have two lemon thymes (*Thymus citriodrus*) that are quite different even in growth habit. My original lemon thyme is a creeper that forms mats about 3 inches high. The later one is an upright plant, like garden thyme, but with larger, lemon-scented leaves and a lower habit of growth.

One problem with thyme that is especially true of common thyme is that it tends to get woody, like a small shrub rather than a forb (the botanist's term for nonwoody plants that are not grasses; confusingly, often called herbs). One way to prevent this is to cut your plant back every spring almost to the ground. The new shoots will be soft and easy to chop for cooking purposes.

Thyme is seldom used alone as a flavoring. It mixes so well with other herbs and flavors that it is frequently combined with bay, parsley, oregano, garlic, saffron, and so forth. Since thyme is native to the area around the Mediterranean Sea, it is frequently found in combinations called Provençal, after the land of Provençe which used to be a separate country with its own language, but is now part of the South of France, While Provençal dishes frequently feature tomatoes, the essence is the combination of herbs—thyme, garlic, basil, and often fennel or saffron.

There is a marvelous way to make fried chicken that illustrates this constellation of flavors that does not use the ubiquitous tomato. Heat some oil, butter, or lard in a large, heavy skillet. When the fat is hot, "brown" cut-up pieces of chicken until they have turned yellow (white if you have skinned them first). Remove them and sprinkle them with fresh thyme. Put several cloves of unpeeled garlic in the fat, and return the chicken (remember that the dark meat takes longer to cook than the white, so it should go in first.) Grind pepper on the chicken and add salt if you like. Cook until the juices run clear when a piece is pierced with a fork.

Remove the chicken and cover it with foil.

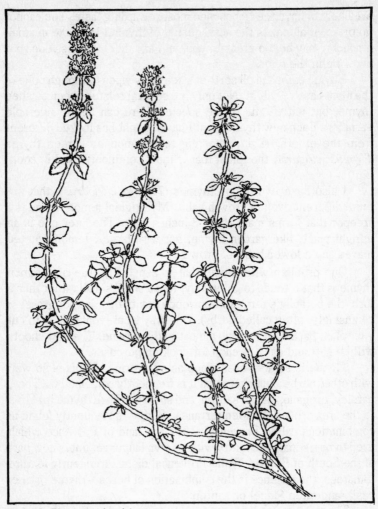

THYME (*Thymus vulgaris*)

Actually, you could stop right at that point and have a creditable fried chicken—but this is a French dish (even if really Provençal), so there is an appropriate sauce. The sauce is made like a mayonnaise or hollandaise, by adding fat or oil to eggs. In this case, the fat is the flavored fat in which the chicken has cooked. First mash the garlic cloves into the fat (removing the skins). Then deglaze the fat with white wine or chicken stock, adding the liquid to the pan and turning the heat up. The flavor will be more authentic if you add a little fennel to the liquid. As the wine or stock boils, use a wooden spoon to scrape up the bits of browned chicken and herbs that have stuck to the bottom of the pan. After the bits have all been scraped up, put a spoonful of chopped basil in the fat and liquid.

Now beat one or two eggs until they are fairly thick. The easiest way to do this is in a food processor. Pour in the fat a little at a time, as you continue beating, and the sauce is formed. It should not be as thick as mayonnaise, since there will be less fat in it, but it should be like heavy cream. You may want to heat the sauce slightly before pouring it over the chicken.

WINTER SAVORY

I was disturbed to read in Waverly Root's last book on food that no one uses winter savory today, since I use it regularly all summer. Of course, some summers I do grow summer savory; in those summers, since summer savory is somewhat of a rarity in the garden, the summer variety gets the nod over the winter savory. But those summers become rarer and rarer, since I find no noticeable advantage in summer savory over winter.

Although they are of the same genuis and the same general flavor, no one looking at the plants from any distance would connect winter savory (*Satureia montana*) and summer savory (*Satureia hortensis*). In overall form, summer savory looks a lot like marjoram, while winter savory resembles garden thyme. Also, winter savory is a much darker green than summer savory. A closer look shows the savory family traits and the differences from either marjoram or thyme. Both savories have the same kind of flowers and—although the leaves of winter savory are smaller—the same shaped leaves. Summer savory, however, is an upright plant that is extremely narrow in form, while winter savory is a low bush. Also, although the leaves are the same shape, those of winter savory are, as is often the case with perennials adapted to harsher climates, not only smaller but more spiky—somewhat like conifer needles, in fact, for the same water-preserving reasons that conifers generally have needles instead of flat leaves. The flavor of each savory, despite the differences, is so much like the other that either can be readily substituted in any recipe without loss of authenticity.

If I have any complaints about winter savory at all, they are (1) that winter savory tends to spread unless it is contained, (2) in my climate, winter savory does not live up to its name. It loses all its leaves in winter, although they return in the spring. (In milder climates, I have heard that winter savory indeed does stay green all winter, but in our mildest on record, mine went totally dead—for

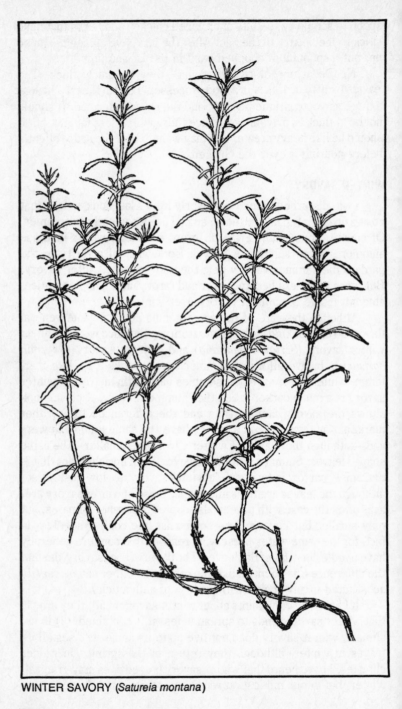

WINTER SAVORY (*Satureia montana*)

the winter only, however.) If it kept its leaves, winter savory would make an excellent low hedge, so long as you did not want a hedge to grow higher than about 1 or 1½ feet. A hedge of winter savory would be blessed with tiny white flowers for most of the summer, which would make up for some deficiencies in size and winter appearance.

Savory in both forms is linked closely with beans, although it is an excellent flavoring for broiled chicken and can replace thyme in many dishes. The authorities tell you to use summer savory with fresh green beans and winter savory with dried bean dishes, but I use winter savory with both.

My favorite way of cooking green beans is a modified version of the French *maître d'hôtel* style. The beans are first blanched in the largest pot of boiling water available or at least the largest pot for which you are willing to wait for the water to come to the boil. As you stem the beans, separate them into three or four piles by size. When the water is boiling vigorously, begin adding the pile of largest beans to the water a handful at a time, trying to keep the water boiling. Continue with beans of decreasing size until all are in the water.

After five or six minutes, start pulling one bean out at a time to taste it. As soon as the beans lose their raw taste, but while they are still crisp, pour the beans into a colander and run cold water over them until they are all cold, shaking the colander from time to time to make sure that all the beans are cooling. (The average time for cooking my beans is around nine minutes—cooling takes a minute or two.) Lay the beans in one layer on paper towels. Roll the towels into cylinders and store in the refrigerator until just before serving.

When you are about ready to serve the beans, shake them out of the paper towels, put them into a large saucepan, and start heating them over a moderately high burner. Shake the pan to keep the beans from sticking. After you think that any excess water has been removed, add a tablespoon of butter and a few drops of lemon juice. Keep shaking. When the butter is melted, repeat with more butter and lemon juice. Keep shaking. When it looks to you as if the butter has formed a sauce on the beans, add a generous quantity of chopped leaves of winter savory. Keep shaking for a moment, then serve.

Chapter 7
Recipes

Many recipes use herbs. This section by no means contains a complete list. Rather it is just a sampling of recipes to get you started (if you are not already) in the use of fresh herbs in cooking. Most French and Italian cookbooks contain many recipes using herbs, as do those of various other ethnic groups.

To make the recipe section more useful, I have used a method for describing ingredients and cooking steps that is based on the normal presentation used in Chinese cooking. That is, the steps are numbered and the ingredients are grouped by step. Each recipe begins with a total preparation time, of which the cooking time is only a part. Following this, there is a list of any special cooking equipment that will be needed, then the list of ingredients needed for each step. Last comes the actual cooking steps themselves. If you have ever used a Chinese cookbook, all this will seem quite natural.

Salt. No salt is used in any of the recipes. If you are accustomed to adding salt, you may miss that flavor, although the herbs make up for the lack of salt in most instances. If you miss the flavor, add salt to taste at the end of cooking the dish.

Amounts. In cooking, you need less of most dried herbs than of fresh ones—except for bay, which can be one-to-one dried to fresh. While the recipes in this section generally specify fresh herbs and provide amounts on that basis, recipes in most cookbooks are generally based on the use of dried leaves or powdered dried leaves. When using another source for a recipe, use the following guidelines: you need about twice as much of a fresh herb as you do of whole dried leaves that are crumbled at the last minute. If a recipe calls for ground herbs or if you suspect that the recipe writer had ground herbs in mind (most do), then you need three times the quantity of fresh herbs. A little arithmetic should suggest that about half again the amount of crumbled dried leaves will substitute for the stated amount of powdered herbs.

Similarly, if you are using the recipes that follow but have to use dried herbs instead of fresh, you can generally reverse the amount guidelines given above. That is, use about one-half as much dried whole leaves as the recipe calls for. Powdered herbs are best avoided, but if you have no choice, use about a third as much of the powder as the recipe calls for.

Timing. While I have no scientific proof that the following procedure is correct, I generally add dried herbs to a recipe sooner than I would add fresh ones (bay is once again an exception). I believe it takes slightly longer for the heat and liquid used in cooking to extract the flavors from dried herbs. In any case, the dried herbs should be thoroughly soaked in the liquid, so even if you add the at the very end of the cooking process (as I would with, say, basil, which is extremely volatile) you should make sure the herbs have enough cooking time to soften.

A rule of thumb on cooking with herbs is that the more aroma the plant has when fresh (and not yet cut or bruised) the less time the herb should cook; the aroma comes from the volatile oils in the herbs. If you can smell an unbruised leaf that is still on the plant, then the herb is giving off its volatiles at that moment. If you cannot smell the herb until a leaf is bruised or cut, the volatiles are a bit more securely bound to the plant. If the herb has no aroma even when cut or bruised, so that you can only obtain the flavor by tasting it, the volatiles are still more tightly bound.

Some herbs can fool you. Garlic, for example, has so much in the way of flavor to offer that it can be cooked for a long time, although you can smell the clove as soon as it is peeled (or even before). The flavor of garlic changes, however, with long cooking. The most volatile oils are lost, but others are retained. For this reason garlic has a different effect when added to a dish early in the cooking, when cooked over a high heat, when cooked over a low heat, when crushed, when chopped, and when cooked in its skin. Each process releases different combinations of flavors.

BASIC COOKING

The basic stocks and dressings so necessary to many delicious dishes are presented here. The recipes take full advantage of the marvelous flavors gained by the use of herbs.

Stocks

Making your own stock is essential if you want to prepare many of the best-tasting dishes; however, you can substitute canned stock in an emergency. Canned stock is most often labeled *broth*.

A simple, all-purpose stock can be used in all recipes, although in beef dishes and some soups you may want to use a brown stock of either meat or poultry. Since even meat bones have gotten to be expensive these days, I most often end up with a stock made just from unbrowned chicken or turkey bones. The basic recipe for unbrowned chicken stock is, therefore, the all-purpose version. Veal or beef bones make a nice addition to the basic chicken stock. Lamb or pork bones have too strong a flavor for most purposes.

Unbrowned Stock

Total Time: 12 hours

Special Equipment: as large a pot as is available, with a cover

1 Chicken or turkey bones and meat and skin scraps from at least one whole bird (or the equivalent amount of parts—necks, wing tips, etc. saved in the freezer) or the same amount of beef bones or any combination of chicken, turkey, and beef bones
A few veal bones (optional)
Enough cold water to cover the bones by at least 2 inches

2 1 bay leaf
4 or 5 sprigs parsley
1 or 2 sprigs thyme
1 or 2 sprigs oregano *or* marjoram (optional)
Several lovage leaves (optional)
2 cloves of garlic, unpeeled
1 teaspoon peppercorns
1 large or 2 small onions studded with cloves*
1 large or 2 small carrots
Top(s) from the carrots (optional)

Leaves from 1 or 2 celery stalks (optional)
Green parts from 1 or 2 leeks (optional)

*To stud an onion with cloves, simply insert a clove into each end of the onion. More cloves than that will give the stock too strong a flavor, one that does not mix well with most dishes.

1. Put **group 1** ingredients together in the pot. Place on a burner, and turn heat on High. When the water is close to boiling, scummy particles will begin to rise to the surface, more of them if you have included the veal. Skim these off with a large tablespoon and discard into a throwaway container. (Do not put the skimmed particles in the sink; they will stick tenaciously to it.)
2. When almost all of the scum has been skimmed, add **group 2** ingredients. Reduce heat to a simmer. Skim a bit more until you have gotten nearly all of the scum. Simmer slowly 8 to 12 hours with the lid on the pot, but askew, so that steam can escape slowly. Strain the liquid into jars.

The broth may be kept for several days in the refrigerator or frozen (or, of course, used immediately). If there is fat on top, leave it there to protect the stock, but remove it before using the stock. If the stock is kept in the refrigerator, especially if there is no fat on top, it may need to be boiled for a few seconds every 3 or 4 days to prevent cloudiness caused by bacteria.

Browned Beef Stock

Total Time: 12½ hours

Special Equipment: roasting pan, wooden spoon, large stock pot

1 3 or 4 pounds beef bones, preferably with some meat attached; shin or neck is good
Veal bones (optional)
2 peeled onions, halved
2 scraped carrots, quartered

2 Enough cold water to cover bones by 2 inches
1 or 2 cups boiling water

3 1 fresh bay leaf
4 or 5 sprigs parsley
1 or 2 sprigs thyme

1 or 2 sprigs oregano *or* marjoram (optional)
Several lovage leaves (optional)
2 cloves of garlic, unpeeled
1 teaspoon peppercorns
1 large or 2 small onions studded with cloves
1 large or 2 small carrots
Top(s) from the carrots (optional)
Leaves from 1 or 2 celery stalks (optional)
Green parts from 1 or 2 leeks (optional)

1. Preheat oven to 350°F. Place **group 1** ingredients in the roasting pan. Roast in the oven, turning ingredients every 5 or 6 minutes, until meat is all browned.

2. Pour off the fat from the roasting pan and put the **group 1** ingredients into a stock pot with the cold water (**group 2**). There should be brown bits sticking to the pan. Add boiling water to the roasting pan and place the pan over a high heat. With a wooden spoon, scrape all the browned bits from the bottom of the pan, which should color the boiling water in the pan a rich brown. When you have all the brown bits scraped into the water (or almost all—it's hard to get all of it), add the boiling water to the stock pan. Skim off the scummy particles (see preceding Unbrowned Stock recipe).

3. When almost all of the scum has been skimmed; add **group 3** ingredients. Reduce heat to a simmer. Skim a bit more until you have gotten nearly all of the scum. Simmer slowly for 8 to 12 hours with the lid on the pot, but askew, so that steam can escape slowly. Strain the liquid into jars.

The broth may be kept for several days in the refrigerator or frozen (or, of course, used immediately). If there is fat on top, leave it there to protect the stock but remove it before using the stock. If the stock is kept in the refrigerator, especially if there is no fat on top, it may need to be boiled for a few seconds every 3 or 4 days.

Brown Poultry Stock

Total Time: 12¼ hours

Special Equipment: large frying pan, large stock pot

1 Chicken or turkey bones and meat scraps from at least 1 whole bird (or an equivalent amount of parts saved in the freezer)
Enough cooking oil (peanut oil preferred) to cover bottom of frying pan.

2 Enough cold water to cover bones by at least 2 inches
1 or 2 cups boiling water

3 1 fresh bay leaf
4 or 5 sprigs parsley
1 or 2 sprigs thyme
1 or 2 sprigs oregano *or* marjoram (optional)
Several lovage leaves (optional)
2 cloves of garlic, unpeeled
1 teaspoon peppercorns
1 large or 2 small onions studded with cloves
1 large or 2 small carrots
Top(s) from the carrots (optional)
Leaves from 1 or 2 celery stalks (optional)
Green parts from 1 or 2 leeks (optional)

    1. If bones and scraps (**group 1**) were frozen, let thaw and wipe dry. Heat the oil (**group 1**) until almost smoking. Brown the bones and meat scraps in the oil.
    2. Pour off the oil from the frying pan, add the bones to the stock pot with the cold water (**group 2**), and proceed to scrape up the browned bits as in **step 2** for preceding Browned Beef Stock recipe. Add the boiling water to the stock pot.
    3. When almost all of the scum has been skimmed, add **group 3** ingredients. Reduce heat to a simmer. Skim a bit more until you have gotten nearly all of the scum. Simmer slowly for 8 to 12 hours with the lid on the pot, but askew, so that steam can escape slowly. Strain the liquid into jars.
    The broth may be kept for several days in the refrigerator or frozen (or, of course, used immediately). If there is fat on top, leave it there to protect the stock but remove it before using the stock. If the stock is kept in the refrigerator, especially if there is no fat on top, it may need to be boiled for a few seconds every 3 or 4 days to prevent cloudiness caused by bacteria.

Herbal Mayonnaise

    Herbal mayonnaise sometimes called green mayonnaise, is best used with fish dishes—notably hot or cold poached salmon. I like mayonnaise made with dill especially for salmon, but other combinations of green herbs are also excellent. (Watch out for coriander, though. It can be rather strong in mayonnaise if used too lavishly.) Basil, chives, parsley, and fennel also make excellent mayonnaises, either alone or in combination with each other or with dill.

You probably can make a herbal mayonnaise by chopping the herbs and mixing them into a good commercial mayonnaise, but I have never tried it. Homemade mayonnaise is easy to make—especially with a food processor—and has more the texture of a sauce. Commerical mayonnaise is a good consistency for spreading on bread, but it is too thick to dip a chunk of poached salmon in.

If you do not have a food processor, chop all the herbs very fine and be prepared to beat the mayonnaise quite a bit.

Total Time: 1 hour

Special Equipment: food processor

1 Several tablespoons herb leaves, either all dill, or a mixture of dill and parsley, or basil and parsley, or chives and parsley, or whatever suits your fancy

2 1 egg, preferably at room temperature
1 tablespoon lemon juice
1 tablespoon mustard, if desired

3 1¼ cups oil (good-quality olive oil mixed with either safflower oil or sunflower oil is recommended)

1. Chop the **group 1** ingredients, using the steel blade of the food processor. Leave the herbs and the steel blade in the processor for the rest of the preparation.
2. Add **group 2** ingredients. Process until thoroughly blended, about 15 seconds.
3. Trickle ¼ cup of the oil (**group 3**) into the processor as it continues running. On some food processors there is a special small hole through which oil can be added that will allow the oil to trickle at just the right speed. It might take as much as a minute to add the ¼ cup, but this is just right. The remaining cup of oil can be added at a faster pace. When all the oil has been added, the mayonnaise should be done. Chill for a while before serving. The mayonnaise will keep in a covered jar for several days in the refrigerator.

Green Sauce
This herb sauce for cold meat, cold chicken, or cold shellfish is basically the same as herbal mayonnaise, but green sauce is more of a sauce than a mayonnaise.

Special Equipment: food processor or blender

1 1 cup parsley
½ cup chives
¼ cup basil leaves
¼ cup thyme leaves
1 shallot *or* 2 or 3 Egyptian onions bulbils
1 teaspoon lemon juice

2 1 cup homemade mayonnaise (use the Herbal Mayonnaise recipe but omit all herbs)

1. With the food processor, chop **group 1** ingredients fine. If you use a blender, you may have to chop the herbs by hand first, then blend. You may also need to add a tablespoon of oil to get them to blend in the blender.

2. Add the mayonnaise (**group 2**) and process or blend thoroughly. Chill before serving.

Basic Tomato Sauce

This is more a pasta sauce than a simple tomato sauce that you would use with meatloaf or as an ingredient in a veal or chicken recipe. It can be varied in many different ways, for many different purposes, simply by varying the herbs used. For example, I like a little rosemary in a sauce for pasta, but I would omit both the rosemary and oregano for a French tomato sauce. Use a lot of oregano, thyme, and basil, and you have pizza sauce. Add cumin and more garlic and more oregano, and knock out the thyme—you have the basis of a good chili, needing only more onions, meat, hot peppers, and (perhaps) beans to complete the dish. Also, there are two different textures you can make, simply by either pureeing the sauce in a food processor at the end or not. The rough texture works well for pasta sauce, chili, and pizza, while the smooth texture is better for French dishes.

Total Time: ½ hour; better if you can simmer it for several hours

Special Equipment: wooden spoon, large saucepan, food processor (if desired)

1 2 tablespoons olive oil
2 medium-to-large onions, chopped
2 peppers, either both sweet or one sweet and one hot, chopped
1 carrot, shredded
Several grinds of pepper
2 cloves of garlic, smashed, peeled, and chopped

2 4 or 5 large tomatoes, peeled and seeded
     or 1 large can peeled plum tomatoes plus fresh tomato,
     peeled and seeded
1 cup stock
½ cup red wine
1 strip dried or fresh orange peel
1 fresh bay leaf

3 Dash hot pepper flakes
½ teaspoon fresh oregano (double or triple for pizza or chili)
¼ teaspoon fresh rosemary (omit for anything but pasta)
½ teaspoon fresh thyme
Pinch saffron, if available

4 1 tablespoon chopped basil leaves
1 tablespoon softened butter, if you are allowed

    1. The timing works about right if you add the **group 1** ingredients in the order listed, cooking each while preparing the next to be added. Be sure not to overheat the oil while you are chopping the onions. The tomatoes should be peeled and seeded before you begin, however, or the garlic will overcook. Use a moderate heat under the large saucepan. Add the chopped onions to the oil, stirring once or twice with the wooden spoon. The saucepan can be uncovered. As the onions cook, core, seed, and chop the peppers. Red sweet peppers make the nicest sauce for most dishes, but I like to substitute one hot pepper for pasta, and green peppers are almost as good. Add the peppers and, while they are cooking, peel and shred the carrot with a grater or with the food processor. Put in several grinds of black pepper. Finally, mash the garlic with the flat of a knife, peel, and chop. Have the tomatoes handy, because the garlic should cook for only a few seconds. After only a few seconds in hot oil, stop the sautéing process with the addition of some kind of liquid.
    2. Add **group 2** ingredients and cook for a while. The amount

of cooking at this point depends on how big a hurry you are in. If you want tomato sauce in half an hour, cook for 5 minutes. If you can wait a while, simmer for 2 or 3 hours. From time to time, mash the tomatoes with the back of the wooden spoon.

3. Fifteen or 20 minutes before the sauce is to be used (or stored for future use), add **group 3** ingredients. Continue to simmer the sauce.

4. Shortly before serving, add **group 4** ingredients and swirl around in the sauce. This step may be delayed until serving even if the sauce is refrigerated for several days or frozen.

Bearnaise Sauce

One of the great sauces for steak (and other kinds of meat, fish, and chicken) is the essence of tarragon made into a rich sauce. Bearnaise sauce is somewhat like a mayonnaise, but butter is the fat used instead of oil, therefore, bearnaise is in the hollandaise family instead of the mayonnaise family. (Hollandaise sauce is not treated here, since it has no herbs in it.) Bearnaise is very good, although not very good for you.

Total Time: ½ hour

Special Equipment: food processor

1 ¼ cup wine vinegar
  ¼ cup dry white wine
  1 tablespoon peeled, finely chopped Egyptian onion bulbils
  ¼ cup tarragon leaves
  1 or 2 grinds of black pepper

2 3 sticks butter

3 3 egg yolks

4 2 tablespoons tarragon leaves
  1 tablespoon chopped parsley

1. Combine **group 1** ingredients in a small saucepan and boil gently until reduced to two tablespoons of liquid. (It will look like more than that because of the solids.) Strain the liquids through a sieve, pressing to reove the liquid, and let the cook liquid cool in a small bowl. Discard the solids.

2. While the liquid is cooling, melt the butter (**group 2**) in the same saucepan over a slow fire. Add the egg yolks (**groups 3**) to the bowl of a food processor fitted with the steel blade, and process for 1½ minutes. Then turn the fire up to bring the butter to a boil. Watch out for spatters.

3. Dribble the butter slowly into the egg yolks with the processor running. The sauce should thicken the way that mayonnaise does. When all the butter has been added, stop the processor. Add the liquid from **step 1** to the sauce, and pulse the processor on and off to mix thoroughly.

4. Add **group 4** ingredients to the sauce, and process until the herbs are finely chopped. Serve at room temperature.

STARTERS
Judith's Guacamole

This can be a cocktail dip, start a Mexican meal, or replace a salad at a meal. The recipe makes about 3 cups, enough for a small dinner party as a dip. It will keep if covered with plastic wrap, but darkens if exposed to air.

Total Time: 10 minutes
Serves six as a salad

1 1 medium onion, chopped
2 medium tomatoes, chopped

2 2 medium, very ripe avocados
lemon juice to taste

3 2 or more hot peppers, either canned jalapeños or fresh, with seeds and ribs removed, chopped

4 Chopped fresh coriander leaves to taste

1. Mix **group 1** ingredients.
2. Mash the avocados (**group 2**) with a fork and add the lemon juice (**group 2**). Mix thoroughly with onion/tomato mixture.
3. Add the chopped peppers (**group 3**), tasting frequently to adjust for hotness. Two canned peppers are about right for most people. Fresh peppers may be either hotter or less hot, depending on the variety and the particular pepper (hotness varies even on the same plant).

174

4. Several tablespoons of coriander (**group 4**) adds an au thentic touch, but there are some people who do not′like the taste o↑ coriander, so if you do not know your audience you might want to use less.

Cheese Spread

If it were not for the butter, this beer garden speciality would be low in calories. However, were it not for the butter . . .

Total Time: 5 minutes
Serves six

Special Equipment: food processor

1 1 small onion

2 2 teaspoons anchovy paste
2 teaspoons dry mustard
1 cup cottage cheese
1 stick unsalted butter

3 1 tablespoon caraway seeds
1 tablespoon pickled nasturtium buds *or* capers

1. Chop the onion (**group 1**) finely with the steel blade of the food processor.
2. Add **group 2** ingredients, and process until smooth. Remove from mixing bowl of processor and put in regular mixing bowl.
3. Blend in **group 3** ingredients. Chill until ready to serve on crackers.

Mushrooms á la Grecque

I still remember the first time I ever had these, at the Auberge Brettone in Putnam County, New York. It was the start of the last meal of a gastronomic tour of New England taken by my wife and I and a couple of very close friends. Since then, I have tried to recapture the concept of the dish as served that day. Here is a version that makes heavy use of several fresh and dried herbs that comes close to what I remember. Still, you probably had to be there.

Total Time: 12 hours
Serves six

1 1½ pounds mushrooms

2 2 cups water
1 cup olive oil
Juice of 3 lemons
1 tablespoon chopped lovage leaves
1 clove of garlic, crushed and chopped
1 tablespoon chopped fennel leaves
1 teaspoon chopped chervil
Leaves from 4 sprigs thyme
1 bay leaf
¾ teaspoon coriander seed, ground
8 peppercorns

  1. If the mushrooms (**group 1**) are, as usual, of widely varying sizes, cut the larger ones in half or quarters so that the results are fairly uniform.
  2. Combine the mushrooms with **group 2** ingredients in a small saucepan and bring to a boil. Reduce heat and simmer for 5 minutes, stirring from time to time. Remove the mushrooms and herbs. Boil the cooking liquid until it has reduced to 1 cup. Return the mushrooms and herbs to the saucepan. Place the contents of the saucepan in a bowl, cover with plastic wrap, and allow to marinate overnight in the refrigerator. Serve at room temperature for the best flavor.

SOUPS
Quick Clam Chowder for Two

  Since my wife and I both work at home, we like to cook our "lunch for two." In the winter, our most common lunch is a filling soup—especially one fairly low in calories and fat. Since we nearly always have stock on hand, most of the soup is based on that, although occasionally I make big batches of bean soup (without stock) for pasta fazool.
  We nearly always have on hand the key ingredients for a quick clam chowder. This is not a chowder for company, which should be made from scratch with fresh clams, raw potatoes, and cream, but just a light lunch that can be put together in a half hour.
  It utilizes any suitable leftover vegetables in the refrigerator, and is intended to be the whole lunch, except maybe for a piece of fruit for dessert. In fact, it makes rather more lunch than two people of normal appetites would want. We usually have some left over. If

bread or crackers accompany it, the soup, along with a salad and a more substantial dessert could be lunch for three or four people instead of just two.

Cooking Time: ½ hour

1 1 medium to large onion, chopped
Several grinds of pepper
1 tablespoon butter *or* margarine
½ teaspoon chopped fresh thyme

2 1 cup (1 8-ounce bottle) clam juice
2 cups stock
½ cup white wine
2 or 3 drops Tabasco hot pepper sauce
Small pinch saffron *or* large pinch tumeric

3 ½ cup leftover sliced carrots *or* whole corn
1 or 2 baked or boiled potatoes, peeled and diced

4 1 8-oz. can chopped clams with the liquid
1 cup milk

1. Cook the onion and pepper (**group 1**) in the butter or margarine (**group 1**) in a medium saucepan until the onion is soft. Add the thyme (**group 1**).

2. Add the liquids (**group 2**). Season with Tabasco hot pepper sauce and saffron or tumeric (**group 2**) and bring to a simmer.

3. Add **group 3** ingredients and bring to a simmer again.

4. Add the **group 4** ingredients. Bring almost to a simmer, correct seasoning if needed, and serve.

Westchester Clam Chowder

Westchester is between Manhattan and New England, so this is a cross between white, creamy New England Clam Chowder (which is like the Quick Clam Chowder for Two, above) and tomato-based Manhattan Clam Chowder. In fact, it is just the recipe given above with enough tomato sauce (see Basic Tomato Sauce, page 171) added to give a good color—three or four tablespoons should do.

Pistou

Pistou is really the name of a French paste that is similar to

177

Italian pesto. The soup itself is similar to Italian pasta fazool. It can be made with either dried, canned, or fresh beans. If you use dried beans, they should be cooked and added in **step 2**, while canned beans, which do not need to be cooked, should also be added at that step. This version is for fresh shelled beans. It also uses unshelled green beans (I recommend the flat Italian variety).

As you can see, this is a French dish that is almost Italian.

Cooking Time: 1 hour
Serves six

Special Equipment: food processor

1 6 cups water
1 cup diced carrots
1 cup diced potatoes
1 cup diced onions
1 cup shelled beans

2 1 cup diced green beans
½ cup ditalini *or* spaghetti broken into short pieces
½ cup bread crumbs
Pinch of saffron *or* tumeric

3 4 cloves of garlic, mashed
4 tablespoons tomato paste
¼ cup chopped basil
½ cup Parmesan cheese
¼ cup olive oil

1. Bring water to boiling and add vegetables (**group 1**). Return to a slow boil for about 40 minutes.

2. Add **group 2** ingredients and boil slowly for about 15 minutes, until the pasta is cooked to your taste. At that time, if all has gone well, all the vegetables should be done.

3. Place **group 3** ingredients, except the olive oil, in the food processor, and, using the steel blade, chop into a paste. Drizzle in the olive oil while continuing to process, forming a thick sauce. Add a cup of the soup, including the vegetables, and process some more. Empty the contents of the food processor into the soup and mix well.

Black Bean Soup

There are many people who think this is the basic idea of what soup should be.

Total Time: 3 or 4 hours
Serves six as a lunch dish

Special Equipment: food processor or food mill

1 1½ cups dried black turtle beans
1½ quarts stock
1 tablespoon oil

2 1 medium onion, chopped
1 tablespoon oil
1 carrot including leaves, grated and chopped
1 potato, grated
Several grinds of pepper
1 clove of garlic, crushed and chopped
1 bay leaf

3 1 teaspoon chopped lovage leaves
1 teaspoon chopped oregano leaves
½ teaspoon chopped winter savory leaves

4 ½ lemon, thinly sliced
Dash of sherry per serving

1. Put washed black beans in the stock and oil **(group 1)**, bring to a boil, and simmer for about 2½ hours until beans are tender.

2. Sauté onion in oil **(group 2)** in a separate skillet, while preparing other vegetables **(group 2)** until onion is translucent. Add carrot, potato, and pepper and sauté for 2 or 3 minutes. Add garlic and bay leaf **(group 2)**. After a few seconds, empty contents of skillet into pot with the beans.

3. After the beans and vegetables have cooked for about 15 minutes, add **group 3** ingredients. Cook for another 15 minutes or so until the beans and the vegetables are done. Put the soup in a food processor with the steel blade or through the medium insert of a food mill.

179

4. Reheat the soup. Float slices of lemon (**group 4**) in bowls of soup and just before serving add sherry (**group 4**) to taste

FISH AND SEAFOOD
Linguine with White Clam Sauce

I got interested in this dish when a disk jockey I used to listen to would announce every day around noon that he was starved, and that his hunger could be satisfied only by a dish of linguine with white clam sauce. After hearing this many times, I saw the dish on a menu and tried it. Terrific! Unfortunately, I am the only one in the family who feels this way. Therefore, the following recipe is for one serving. Simply multiply by the number of people to get the amount for your group. (Actually, I am quite generous with the clams for myself. If you wanted to stretch a single can of clams for two people, just multiply everything else by two but the clams.)

Total Time: 20 minutes

Special Equipment: a large and a small saucepan

1 3 or 4 quarts water
¼ pound dried linguine

2 1 tablespoon butter
1 tablespoon olive oil

3 1 large or 2 small cloves of garlic, chopped
Several grinds of black pepper
Pinch of red pepper flakes
1 teaspoon chopped fresh oregano
¼ cup chopped parsley
2 tablespoons dry white wine
1 6½-ounce can of chopped clams, undrained

1. Put the water (**group 1**) on to boil in the large saucepan and continue with **step 2** of the recipe. When the water is boiling, add the linguine (**group 1**) a little at a time, keeping the water at a boil. Boil the linguine for about 10 minutes, testing toward the end by biting off the end of a strand to make sure that it is cooked as you like it.

2. As soon as the water goes on the stove, melt the butter in the olive oil (**group 2**) in the small saucepan.

3. Add the **group 3** ingredients to the **group 2** ingredients in the order listed, chopping as you go along. Simmer until the linguine is cooked, drained, and turned into a soup bowl. Pour the clam sauce over the linguine, toss, and eat while drinking a chilled glass of the dry white wine. (Frascati is nice with this.)

Coquilles Provençale

While this can be a first course, it also makes an excellent lunch or light supper.

Total Time: 20 to 25 minutes
Serves four for lunch
or six as a starter

Special Equipment: skillet, scallop shells or small ovenproof dishes

1 1½ pounds bay scallops
1 cup flour mixed with a few grinds of pepper

2 1 tablespoon butter
1 small onion, chopped fine
5 or 6 Egyptian onions bulbils, peeled and chopped
1 clove of garlic, crushed and chopped

3 ⅔ cup dry white wine
1 bay leaf
1 sprig thyme, leaves removed and chopped (about ½ teaspoon chopped leaves)

4 ¼ cup grated swiss cheese

1. Dredge the scallops thoroughly in the flour (**group 1**), shake off the excess, and leave on waxed paper while you cook the onions (**step 2**). Turn the oven on broil.

2. Melt the butter and sauté the onion while you chop the Egyptian onions (**group 2**). Add the Egyptian onions and stir, then crush and chop the garlic (**group 2**). Add the garlic, then the scallops and cook them for a couple of minutes until they are golden.

3. Add **group 3** ingredients to the skillet and cover it. Simmer for 5 minutes, then remove the cover and boil down the sauce slightly. Remove the bay leaf and discard.

4. Place the scallops in four scallop shells for a lunch or supper, in six scallop shells as a starter. Sprinkle with the cheese

181

(group 4) and run under the broiler until the cheese is melted and slightly browned. Serve with a chilled pouilly fumé.

Herbed Fillets of Flounder

I grew up on fried catfish. This is a way to take some of the essential ideas behind that popular Midwestern dish and refine them somewhat (without omitting the caloric content, which is heavy in either case). You do not need tartar sauce for this one.

Total Time: 1 hour
Serves four

Special Equipment: skewers, food processor or blender, two paper plates, cookie sheet

1 1 stick butter

2 About 8 flounder fillets

3 2 tablespoons peeled, minced Egyptian onion bulbils
1 teaspoon chopped tarragon leaves
1 tablespoon chopped parsley
½ teaspoon chopped thyme *or* (preferably) lemon thyme leaves
1 tablespoon lemon juice
1 pinch of pepper, preferably white

4 2 eggs
2 teaspoons cooking oil
2 tablespoons water

5 Flour
2 cups bread crumbs, made in food processor or blender

6 ¼ cup melted butter

    1. Cut the butter **(group 1)** into pieces and set it out to soften.
    2. Turn the fillets **(group 2)** so their milky side is up, and use a sharp knife to scored diamonds on that side. This will prevent the fish from curling the wrong way during cooking.
    3. Add **group 3** ingredients to the butter and beat until the result is creamy and thoroughly mixed.
    4. Beat the eggs with the oil and water **(group 4)**. Spread

some of the herb butter on each fillet until they all have received an equal amount. Roll the fillets up like jellyrolls, and thread them on the skewers. You can put four on a skewer, or, if you prefer, only two per skewer, since two fillets feed one person.

5. Put the flour and the bread crumbs (**group 5**) in separate paper plates. Roll the skewered and buttered fillets in flour. Shake extra flour back into the paper plate, then dip the fillets in the egg mixture. Again shake off the extra. Now roll the fillets in the bread crumbs. Press the crumbs slightly with your hand to make them stay on the fish. Put the fish on a waxed paper-covered cookie sheet as you finish each skewer. When all the fish have been thoroughly coated, put the fish—still on the waxed paper—into the refrigerator for at least half an hour, for the coating to firm up.

6. Slide the waxed paper and fillets off the cookie sheet, and butter the cookie sheet. Put the fillets on the sheet, and brush their tops with the melted butter (**group 6**). Broil under a medium broiler for about 5 minutes (watching closely to see that the topping doesn't burn), then turn and baste again. Broil for another 5 minutes and serve. Try a chilled dry Riesling with the fish.

POULTRY
Italian Fried Chicken

There is no end to ways to make fried chicken. While the traditional American way uses few or no herbs, many of the European versions have strong herbal flavors. The version that uses thyme, basil, and garlic and comes with a sauce is presented under "Thyme" in the "Encounters with Herbs" chapter. Here is a version that I discovered once when my wife was on a trip with our two younger children, so it was cooked just for our older son and me. It is flavored entirely with rosemary, a herb that my wife finds too piney in large amounts, although it is one of my favorites. If you really like rosemary, you will love this one; if you do not, try the one with thyme, basil, and garlic.

Total Time: 4 hours

Special Equipment: electric deep-fat fryer or cast-iron chicken fryer (a heavy frying pan, 4 to 5 inches deep)

1 As much chicken as you want to cook, cut up in serving pieces

2 ½ cup olive oil and 1 tablespoon chopped rosemary leaves for each pound of chicken; salt if desired

183

3 Enough good cooking oil (peanut oil is especially good) to make at least 1 inch depth in your fryer

1. Place the chicken pieces (**group 1**) in a bowl with **group 2** ingredients and marinate (soak) them for at least 3 hours.

2. Start heating the cooking oil (**group 3**) in the fryer. While it is heating, wipe the rosemary leaves off the chicken with a paper towel, and discard the towel. Any olive oil that remains can be added to the oil heating in the fryer (with the rosemary strained out).

3. When the oil is almost smoking, fry the chicken, a few pieces at a time so they are not crowded. Turn them from time to time, until they are uniformly golden brown. Remove to drain on a brown paper bag. If you are not sure the chicken is done, pierce one of the larger pieces from the first batch with a fork to see if the juices run clear. If the juices are even slightly pink, you have not fried the chicken enough, and it should be returned to the hot oil for another few minutes. Total frying time will depend on how hot your oil is, but it should be less than 20 minutes.

4. When all the chicken has been fried, it is ready to serve. If there are going to be more than three batches to be fried, you might want to keep the first batches warm in a 300°F oven. The paper bag will not catch fire at that temperature. Serve the chicken with chilled soave.

Chicken Cous Cous

This is an infinitely variable dish that can use up a lot of different vegetables as well as either uncooked or cooked chicken. Amounts do not matter much either, although I'll give suggestions. The amounts given here make a generous dinner for two (along with a green salad). For lunch for four, you might use about the same amount of everything except the cous cous cereal, which should be doubled.

Total Time: 45 minutes
Serves four for Lunch
or two for Dinner

Special Equipment: three saucepans, sieve, bulb baster

1 1 pound chicken, cut into medium-size cubes
2 tablespoons cooking oil

2 1 teaspoon ground cumin
½ teaspoon tumeric
1 teaspoon grated ginger root
Several grinds of pepper

3 1 medium onion, diced
2 ribs celery, cut into large dice
2 medium carrots, sliced
1 bell pepper, cubed (that is, cut into quarter-size pieces)
1 medium zucchini, sliced
2 small to medium turnips, cubed to match chicken (optional)

4 2 cloves of garlic, finely chopped
Hot pepper flakes to taste
1 medium-size can Italian plum tomatoes
2 cups chicken broth

5 1 cup instant cous cous cereal

6 1 tablespoon hot pepper flakes
1 tablespoon cooking oil
½ tablespoon ground coriander seed
½ tablespoon finely chopped ginger root

1. In the largest saucepan, cook the chicken in the oil (**group 1**) until it has turned completely white.

2. Add the **group 2** ingredients to the chicken and stir until the chicken is completely coated and has turned yellow (from the tumeric). Remove the chicken from the pan to an inverted lid, leaving the residue of the oil and flavorings in the saucepan.

3. Put the **group 3** ingredients in the saucepan, cooking over a medium heat as you go. That is, cook each ingredient from the time it goes into the saucepan until all the ingredients have been added. (Total time, then, is about 10 minutes for the onions, with shorter times for each of the other vegetables.)

4. Add the garlic (**group 4**) and remove the saucepan for a moment while you add the hot pepper flakes (**group 4**). The idea is that the garlic should just barely cook and the pepper flakes should cook a little less. (Too-brown garlic or burned pepper flakes can impart a bitter taste to the final dish.) Add the tomatoes (**group 4**) and return to the fire. Add the stock (**group 4**). Simmer until the carrots are just barely tender. Leave on to simmer for a few minutes longer while you prepare the cous cous cereal and the hot sauce.

5. Add the cous cous cereal (**group 5**) to the medium-size saucepan. Put a sieve into the simmering chicken and vegetables to separate the liquid from the solids. With the bulb baster, remove 2 cups of liquid. Leave the chicken and vegetable simmering in the liquid that is left. Over a medium heat, stir the cous cous cereal and the removed liquid until the liquid is absorbed (about 2 minutes) and you have something that looks rather like thick, orange cream-of-wheat. Turn off the heat, cover the saucepan, and let sit at least 10 minutes. This is important, since if you do not wait that long, the cereal will be gummy.

6. While you wait for the cereal to rest, check the vegetables. Taste each one to see if it is tender, or just check the carrots, which are usually the last to cook (although that depends on how thinly they have been sliced). If the vegetables are done, turn off the fire; otherwise, keep simmering. Meanwhile, make the sauce. Combine **group 6** ingredients with about 3 tablespoons of the liquid from the simmering vegetables and chicken and bring briefly to a boil. Set aside until the cereal has rested and the vegetables are tender. Serve by putting a portion of the cereal topped with the chicken and vegetables on each plate. Pass the sauce separately, so that each person can adjust the heat for themselves. (The leftover sauce can be kept for quite some time in a covered jar to be used as a base for the sauce for your next cous cous.) Serve with beer.

MEAT
Lamb with Garlic

Lamb stew is a basic dish that can be varied in many ways. Essentially, the lamb here is a stew without added vegetables. In this recipe, garlic is added at the end, not at the beginning. The result is entirely different from beginning with browned garlic or cooking unbrowned garlic along with the lamb. Serve with a full-bodied red wine such as a barolo.

Total Time: 1½ hours
Serves six to eight

Special Equipment: enameled cast-iron casserole with lid, 4-cup measuring cup or heatproof bowl, medium saucepan

1 2 tablespoons butter *or* margarine
2 tablespoons olive oil

2 4 pounds lamb cut for stew (a mixture of shoulder, breast, and neck, or any two, has the best flavor)
Freshly ground pepper to taste

3 2 large onions, chopped

4 1 cup red wine

5 ¼ cup flour
2 bay leaves
2 sprigs fresh thyme
4 cups brown meat stock

6 ¼ cup parsley chopped with 6 to 8 cloves of smashed and peeled garlic

1. Preheat oven to 375°F. Melt butter or margarine in oil (**group 1**) in casserole and heat until almost smoking.

2. Brown lamb (**group 2**) thoroughly on all sides in fat, grinding in some pepper (**group 2**) from time to time. Remove meat to the inside of the inverted casserole lid.

3. Cook onions (**group 3**) over a lower heat in casserole until translucent. Pour off all but a tablespoon of the browning fat.

4. Deglaze the pan with red wine (**group 4**), using the highest temperature available. Lower heat as low as possible, and leave the reduced wine and onions in the casserole.

5. Return the lamb to the casserole along with any juices that have accumulated in the lid. Sprinkle the flour (**group 5**) over the lamb, and stir well until all the pieces are coated. Cook over a low flame for about 2 minutes, stirring constantly. Add the bay leaves, thyme, and stock (**group 5**). Bring to a medium simmer. Cook, covered, in the middle of the oven for 45 minutes. (Regulate the heat so that the stew is simmering moderately.) Skim the fat as best you can, and continue cooking until lamb is tender—about another half hour.

6. Remove casserole from the oven and pour off juices into a heatproof 4-cup measuring cup or bowl. Remove fat, either by spooning off or by using a bulb baster to remove the liquid below the fat. Put the defatted liquid in a saucepan and boil until somewhat thickened. Return thickened liquid to casserole and add chopped parsley and garlic mixture (**group 6**). Serve with a substantial red wine, such as an Amador-County zinfandel.

FRENCH HAMBURGER

This recipe is different from the hamburger recipe under "Egyptian Onions" in the "Encounter with Herbs" chapter, although like it, it is best served either without a bun or on a slice of toasted French bread. I like having the bread to make sure I get all of the sauce.

Total Time: ½ hour
Three large or four medium burgers

Special Equipment: food processor, mixing bowl, cast-iron skillet, paper plate

1 1 pound lean chuck
1 tablespoon butter
1 teaspoon thyme leaves

2 1 tablespoon butter
½ cup onions

3 1 egg
Several grinds of black pepper

4 1 tablespoon butter
1 tablespoon oil

5 ½ cup flour

6 ½ cup stock
1 tablespoon butter

7 4 slices of French bread, toasted (optional)

1. Chop **group 1** ingredients in the food processor, making sure the meat is ground fine. Remove meat mixture to mixing bowl. Do not rinse processor.

2. Melt butter (**group 2**) in skillet. Meanwhile, chop onions (**group 2**) in food processor until fine. Add onions to skillet and cook slowly until translucent. Add to mixing bowl. Do not clean skillet.

3. Break egg (**group 3**) into mixing bowl and mix thoroughly, adding pepper (**group 3**) from time to time. Form mixture into four patties.

188

4. Melt butter in oil **(group 4)** in skillet.

5. Put flour **(group 5)** on paper plate. Coat patties with flour, shaking off excess. Cook the patties in the skillet over a medium heat, being careful not to burn the flour. The length of time you cook depends on how you like your burgers. Try to turn just once, so you do not lose too much of the coating. Some of the coating will be lost in any case, which will help thicken the sauce.

6. Remove the cooked patties to a warmed plate while you make the sauce. Pour off any fat in the skillet, and deglaze with the stock **(group 6)** over a high heat. When the stock is reduced and has begun to thicken, remove from the heat and add the butter **(group 6)**. Stir it into the sauce until you cannot see it any more. If you are using a bread base, place the burgers on the bread **(group 7)** before pouring the sauce over them. Serve with a beaujolais.

Veal Loaf

The whiteness of veal with the green herbs and peppers makes this an attractive dish. Of course, when you add the tomato sauce, it becomes quite Christmasy.

Total Time: 2 hours
Serves six to eight

Special Equipment: Food processor, 9-inch pie plate, aluminum foil

1 ¾ cup parsley
 ¼ cup chives
 ¼ cup basil leaves
 ½ cup bread
 2 pounds veal for stewing (carefully trimmed)
 2 eggs
 ½ teaspoon freshly ground black pepper
 ¼ cup diced green pepper

2 Bacon slices to cover loaf

3 French-style tomato sauce (see Basic Tomato Sauce, p. 171)

1. Preheat the oven to 350°F. Fill a measuring cup with the parsley, chives, and basil **(group 1)**, mashing them down to make sure the cup is filled. Then chop in the food processor. Add the bread **(group 1)** and process the mixture of herbs and bread into crumbs. Add the veal (**group 1**) and process the whole combination until the veal is finely ground. Add the eggs and pepper (**group 1**) and use the processor for a few seconds to mix. Similarly, add the green peppers (**group 1**) and process for just a few seconds to mix, more than to chop.

2. Remove mixture from the processor and lightly form into a round loaf on a pie plate lined with foil. Cover the loaf with strips of bacon (**group 2**) and bake in the oven for 1½ hours.

3. Slice loaf and serve with tomato sauce (**group 3**). To get the full effect of the colors, make a puddle of sauce and put a slice of veal loaf in the middle. Serve with a California cabernet sauvignon.

Carbonnades

I took up growing herbs because I like to cook. When I first started to cook this was one of my favorite recipes—and it still is. The only problem is what to do with the rest of the 6-pack of beer, but I usually find a suitable way to dispose of it.

Total Time: 4 hours
Serves six to ten,
with leftovers for six

Special Equipment: food processor, enameled iron casserole with lid, 4-cup measuring cup, bulb baster, saucepan

1 2 tablespoons pork fat, trimmed from a roast or chops
1 tablespoon cooking oil, preferably peanut oil
3 pounds chuck or shoulder beef roast, cut into slices about ½ inch thick

2 6 cups sliced onions
Several grinds of black pepper
4 cloves of garlic, mashed and chopped

3 1 cup brown beef stock
2 to 3 cups beer
1 tablespoon brown sugar
6 sprigs parsley
1 bay leaf
2 sprigs thyme

4 1½ tablespoons cornstarch
2 tablespoons wine vinegar

1. Preheat oven to 325°F. In the casserole, cook the pork fat in the oil (**group 1**) until the fat is rendered from the pork. Remove the brown pieces of pork and save for another purpose (such as adding to a salad). Brown the beef slices (**group 1**) and put the browned slices in the lid of the casserole.

2. The food processor should be used to slice the onions, as this is a lot of onions. Brown the onions (**group 2**) in the casserole in the rendered fat, stirring frequently. Add the pepper (**group 2**) when you get time, and add the garlic (**group 2**) just as the onions are browned. Remove the casserole from the heat.

3. Pour off as much of the cooking fat from the onions as you can. Deglaze the casserole with the stock (**group 3**), and scrape the onions over to one side of the casserole. Put ¼ of the beef slices in the other half of the casserole, then move the onions on top of the beef. Put another ¼ of the beef in the empty half of the casserole, and spread the onions over all the beef. Lay the rest of the beef slices on top of the onions. Add enough beer (**group 3**) to cover the beef. Sprinkle the brown sugar (**group 3**) over it all. Use a strong thread to tie the herbs (**group 3**) together in a bundle and bury the herbs in the beer, with the thread left out to retrieve them. Bring the casserole to a simmer on top of the stove, then cover it and put it into the oven for about 1½ hours, or until the meat is very tender.

4. Retrieve the herbs and discard. Pour the liquid from the casserole into the large measuring cup, and let it sit a moment or two while the fat rises to the top. (While this operation is going on, leave the lid on the beef.) Using the bulb baster, extract the fat-free portion of the sauce, and put it in the saucepan over medium heat. While the sauce is boiling lightly, mix the cornstarch and vinegar (**group 4**) and add to the sauce. Simmer until it thickens, stirring constantly. This will take 2 or 3 minutes. Pour any juices that have accumulated in the pan into the sauce as it simmers, then return the thickened sauce to the casserole. Reheat the sauce and meat for a few minutes before serving. If you have not drunk all the beer while cooking, serve with beer.

Veal with Rosemary

This is a very simple veal stew.

Total Time: 45 minutes
Serves four to six

1 1½ pounds veal stew meat, carefully trimmed
2 tablespoons olive oil

2 2 medium onions, chopped
Several grinds of black pepper

3 2 tablespoons flour
¼ cup stock

4 1½ cups tomato juice
1 teaspoon chopped rosemary leaves

    1. Brown the veal in the oil (**group 1**) over a hot fire.
    2. Reduce heat to medium and lightly brown the onions (**group 2**). Add the pepper (**group 2**).
    3. Reduce the heat to low. Sprinkle the flour (**group 3**) over the meat and onions and cook, stirring constantly, for about 2 minutes. Add the stock (**group 3**) and mix carefully so that the flour does not form lumps.
    4. Add the tomato juice and rosemary (**group 4**). Bring to a simmer and simmer until veal is tender. Serve with a chianti classico.

VEGETABLES
Ratatouille

    All the great dishes have infinite variations. Ratatouille is usually listed with the eggplant dishes (and is sometimes called "eggplant casserole with tomatoes" in cookbooks). It is possible, however, to make a perfectly acceptable ratatouille without any eggplant (and with so few tomatoes that they are unnoticeable in the finished dish). Ratatouille is not a recipe, but an idea, like one of those Platonic ideals. Here is how I get close to the ideal when I have all the ingredients I need at hand but do not want to spend the whole day cooking a vegetable stew. (Sometimes I do spend many hours making ratatouille, but such effort is really not necessary unless that is what you feel like doing that day.)

Total Time: 1½ hours
Serves six to eight

Special Equipment: Large, flat, enameled casserole dish, about 12 inches across and 4 inches deep (or frying pan with a lid, around the same size)

1 2 or 3 medium onions, sliced

2 or 3 sweet green or red reppers, cut into quarter-size pieces
1 hot pepper, cut into the same size pieces (or part of one if you
do not like hot pepper much—or omit)
Olive oil to cover bottom of casserole

2 Two cloves of garlic, mashed, peeled, and chopped

3 2 or 3 tablespoons olive oil
1 medium eggplant, cubed with the skin left on
2 or 3 medium zucchini, sliced lengthwise into ⅛-inch slices,
then cut into 1-inch-long pieces

4 2 to 8 peeled, seeded, and chopped tomatoes (depending on how
red and moist you want the dish to be—I generally use 4 or 5
tomatoes)
1 tablespoon caraway seeds (optional)

5 3 to 6 tablespoons basil, parsley, or a mixture of the two (I prefer
a 50-50 mixture)

1. Cook the onions and peppers in the oil (**group 1**) until soft,
but not browned.

2. Add garlic (**group 2**) when onions and pepper are cooked.

3. Add oil (**group 3**) and let it get hot. Then stir in the
vegetables (**group 3**) and cook over moderately high heat until they
begin to brown. The eggplant will "eat" all the oil before the
vegetables get very brown.

4. Reduce heat and add **group 4** ingredients to mixture. Cook
over low heat until liquid begins to form. Baste mixture with liquid
and raise heat to moderate, so that the liquid is boiling. Continue to
baste occasionally or to stir until nearly all of the liquid is gone.

5. Stir in **group 5** ingredients and reduce heat to a simmer.
Simmer, uncovered, for about 20 minutes, basting with the remaining liquid from time to time. Be careful to avoid scorching the
bottom of the stew.

Swiss Chard Pie

The first year I grew swiss chard, I did not know what to do
with it. Of the early experiments, this one worked out the best. In
fact, it is the only one from that year that I am still fond of.

Total Time: 45 minutes
Serves four to six

Special Equipment: pie plate or 8-inch-square pan

1 3 pounds swiss chard (or any large amount)

2 2 cups cottage cheese
2 eggs, beaten
Juice of 1 lemon
2 tablespoons chopped chives

3 2 tablespoons butter *or* margarine

4 ½ cup bread crumbs
Paprika

   1 Preheat oven to 350°F. Remove stems from swiss chard. These can be cooked and eaten separately, rather like asparagus, but they are not nearly so good. I like to cut the stems into short pieces and add them to Chinese stir-fries. Wash and chop leaves roughly, leaving water clinging. Cook quickly in a heavy skillet, stirring constantly until wilted. Put into a sieve and allow to drain.
   2. Beat together the **group 2** ingredients. Take the chard from the sieve and put into a mixing bowl. Take 1 cup of the cottage cheese mixture, and stir it into the chard. Hold the rest in reserve.
   3. Grease the pie plate or pan generously with the butter or margarine (**group 3**). Put the chard/cottage cheese mixture in the pie plate or pan, and press down firmly with a fork until it forms a uniform layer. Spread the rest of the cottage cheese evenly on top.
   4. Sprinkle first with the bread crumbs, then with the paprika (**group 4**). Bake for a half hour or so until the pie is firm.

Spinach-Stuffed Peppers
   If one vegetable is nice, two together can be even better.

Total Time: 25 minutes
Serves four

Special Equipment: steamer

1 4 green bell peppers

2 ½ small yellow onion, chopped
3 tablespoons butter *or* margarine
3 tablespoons flour

3 ¾ cup milk

4 3 quarts spinach or more, chopped

5 1 pinch nutmeg
1 teaspoon chopped basil
1 teaspoon chopped tarragon

6 2 tablespoons bread crumbs mixed with 2 tablespoons grated Parmesan cheese

1. Cut the tops off the peppers (**group 1**), remove the seeds, and scrape out as much of the ribs as you can. Steam the peppers upside down until tender, about 7 minutes.

2. Cook the onion in the butter or margarine (**group 2**) until almost translucent. Add the flour (**group 2**) and cook over a low heat, stirring constantly, for 2 minutes.

3. Add the milk (**group 3**) a little at a time, stirring constantly. The sauce should gradually become thick enough to coat a spoon.

4. Add the spinach (**group 4**) and cook until tender.

5. Stir the **group 5** ingredients into the spinach. Stuff the spinach mixture into the peppers.

6. Place the stuffed peppers in a greased baking dish, spinach side up, and top with the bread crumbs and cheese (**group 6**). If you have excess spinach, place it around the peppers in the dish. Bake for 15 minutes.

BREADS

I generally bake our bread, but most of the time I don't make herb breads, which are too special for general use. Herb breads are, however, wonderful as a special accompaniment to a dinner party. A combination that seems very strange when you first hear of it, but which works wonderfully, is dill bread. I suggest it as a festive bread with fish or with a meat dish that has a strong flavor of its own, such as a hearty stew.

Dill Bread

Total Time: 8-12 hours

Special Equipment: very large bowl, if possible a food processor with special blade for kneading dough, bread board, 1 large or 2 regular bread pans, plastic wrap, pastry brush

1 1 teaspoon dry yeast
⅓ cup tepid water
2 or 3 tablespoons molasses *or* dark syrup

2 2 cups unbleached flour
1½ cups tepid skim milk, preferably soured

3 1½ cups skim milk brought almost to a boil (can be sour)
1 cup instant oatmeal

4 1 teaspoon dry yeast
⅓ cup tepid water
2 or 3 tablespoons molasses *or* dark syrup

5 5 cups unbleached flour
1 or 2 tablespoons oil
2 or 3 tablespoons chopped fresh dill leaves

6 Solid white vegetable shortening to grease baking pan(s)

7 2 or 3 tablespoons water *or* milk *or* beaten egg

    1. Mix **group 1** ingredients, and let stand at least 5 minutes.
    2. Mix **group 2** ingredients, add the yeast mixture, and combine thoroughly. This can be done in the food processor with the plastic bread-making blade. Let stand at least 2½ hours, either in the food processor or in the large bowl.
    3. Bring skim milk (**group 3**) to almost boiling on the stove. Add oatmeal (**group 3**). Let stand until it is tepid.
    4. Mix **group 4** ingredients (the same yeast mixture as before), and again let stand at least 5 minutes.
    5. Add to the yeast/flour/milk mixture 1 cup of flour (**group 5**), mix, another cup of flour, and mix again. Now add the oatmeal mixture (from **step 3**), and mix. Add the dill and mix. Add 3 more cups of flour, mixing after each. By now you should have a heavy dough. Knead either by hand or in the food processor until the dough pulls together in a ball. Put dough in large, oiled bowl, turning it so that the top of the dough is oily. Cover bowl with plastic wrap. Let rise for about 1½ hours, or until doubled in bulk.

6. Empty the bowl onto a lightly floured breadboard. Cut in two pieces if you are making two loaves. Flatten to a thick (½-inch) pancake, fold over, flatten again, fold over again and form into loaves. If using bread pans, they should be greased with white vegetable shortening. Cover bread pans loosely with same plastic wrap that was used before and let rise until doubled in bulk, usually about an hour. If you are not using bread pans, form into a loaf or loaves and let rise on a cookie sheet that has been dusted with cornmeal.

7. Preheat oven to 450°F while bread is rising in pans. Just before putting bread in oven, brush top of loaves with water, milk, or egg. Put bread in oven and turn down to 350°F. If brushing with water, repeat the brushing after a couple of minutes, wait a couple of minutes, and brush for the third time. Bake about 40 to 45 minutes or until it smells like bread. Cool on a rack. While bread can be eaten warm, it should cool at least a bit for best flavor. The bread should be thoroughly cool before wrapping for storage in the refrigerator or freezer.

Rye Bread

Follow the same procedure in the recipe for Dill Bread, but make the following substitutions.

2 Use whole wheat four instead of unbleached white flour.
Tepid water can be substituted for skim milk.

3 Omit these ingredient altogether. Instead, add 1½ cups tepid water in **step 4.**

5 Substitute caraway seed for the dill.
Substitute 3 to 6 cups of rye flour for unbleached white, using white flour for the rest to make a total of 6 cups of flour. The more rye flour, the heavier the bread will be, since rye flour does not rise as well as white.

6 Sprinkle caraway seeds over the tops of the loaves and push into the tops gently before the loaves rise.

Pizza

Homemade pizza is fun to make, good for you, and better than "store-bought." It will astonish your children, since they believe that all pizza emerges from special stores. (Of course, they may still favor the commercial product, but not if they are true gourmets.) This recipe makes two medium pizzas or one large pizza. You can also freeze the dough for later use if you want only one medium pizza. It works better, however, not to try to cut the dough recipe in half, as a smaller amount of dought will not rise properly (the internal temperature does not become high enough for the yeast).

Total Time: 5 hours
Makes one large pizza

Special Equipment: cookie sheet, pizza pan, or special pizza tile; food processor; large bowl; bread board

1 1 teaspoon dry yeast, dissolved in ⅓ cup tepid water

2 4 cups unbleached white or whole wheat flour
1¼ cups tepid water
3 tablespoons olive oil

3 Cornmeal

4 Full recipe for Basic Tomato Sauce with extra oregano and thyme (see page 171)

5 4 cups cheese, preferably mozzarella or a mixture of mozzarella, swiss, Monterey Jack, or cheddar
either
¾ pound mushrooms, sliced
3 tablespoons olive oil
¼ cup nasturtium buds *or* capers
or
½ pound Italian sausage, sliced thin
or
Nothing (for plain pizza)
or
Use whatever combination of toppings you like (add 3 tablespoons olive oil if no fatty meats are included)

6 Chopped oregano leaves
Chopped thyme leaves
Red pepper flakes (optional)

   1. Dissolve the yeast in the water (**group 1**) and mix thoroughly. After five minutes, mix again.

2. Put the flour and water (**group 2**), together with the yeast mixture, in the food processor with the dough-making blade in place. Process until the dough forms a ball. (You may need to stop and scrape some of the flour off the sides of the bowl, then continue processing.) Let the ball rest 2 minutes, then add the olive oil (**group 2**) and process again thoroughly, until all the oil has been absorbed.

Turn out into a large oiled bowl. Cover the bowl with plastic wrap and let dough rise at room temperature until it is at least double or even triple in bulk. The time will vary with the temperature. The best dough is made when the temperature is slightly warmer than room temperature and the rising process takes over 2 hours.

Punch the dough down by poking your fist into the middle, an always-satisfying sensation. Let the dough rise again until it is at least double or even triple in bulk, then punch it down a second time. About a half hour before you think the dough will complete its second rise, start preheating the oven to 450°F. (Start heating the oven somewhat earlier if you are using a pizza tile, which must be heated to get the full effect.)

3. Put the dough on a lightly floured bread board, and cut it in two pieces if you are making two medium pizzas. (Note: one large pizza may strain the capacity of your oven or cooking surface.) Let the dough rest a moment while you rinse out the bowl in which it has risen. If you are going to freeze one of the pieces for later use, wrap it tightly and put it in the freezer. Otherwise, cover it with a plate and weight the plate down to keep it from rising while you make the first pizza. Fold the dough for the first pizza toward the center several times until you have obtained a thick disk. Then flatten it with a floured rolling pin as you would pie dough, until you have a larger disk, but stop for a moment when the dough seems to resist being rolled.

At that point, cover the dough on both sides with a sprinkling of flour and a piece of floured plastic wrap. If you are making two pizzas at a time, transfer your attentions to the other pizza until you reach the same stage. Repeat this process until both pizzas are around 15 inches in diameter and about 3/16 inch thick.

4. Sprinkle your cooking surface with the cornmeal (**group 3**). Transfer the pizza(s) to the cooking surface. If you can simply pick them up and make the move, fine. Otherwise, make sure that the surface is floured and roll each pizza onto the rolling pin for transport, unrolling it carefully onto the cooking surface.

5. Add the tomato sauce **(group 4)** to the top surface of the pizza, trying to cover all parts of the dough.

6. Add the cheese and other toppings **(group 5)**. Opinions vary as to the proper order, but I like to put the other toppings on top of the cheese, since the final result is more attractive. If extra olive oil is needed, sprinkle it on last.

7. Bake for 12 to 15 minutes until all the cheese has melted and the toppings are browned somewhat. If you use sausage, you may have to bake a bit longer to make sure that it is thoroughly cooked. Pass the chopped herbs and red pepper flakes **(group 6)** to be added according to individual tastes.

SALADS

Fresh herbs can be added to many green salads to improve the flavor and bite. I am not talking about some special combination of greens with an exotic dressing, but just a garden-variety combination of lettuce with a wedge of tomato or a few onion rings, topped perhaps with a bottled dressing or a simple homemade vinaigrette. In general, I find that herbs with large, smooth leaves work best in these combinations, although perhaps that is a coincidence. Tarragon, basil, nasturtium, and chives are all terrific. Herbs whose leaves are somewhat rough, such as sage or oregano, or tiny, such as thyme, winter savory, or rosemary, do not blend in with the other ingredients.

Of course there are other things to consider. A herb such as bay is simply too tough to be a part of a salad, while mints or lovage may have too strong a flavor. Chervil, majoram, and parsley are somewhat intermediate.

Garlic is essential for many salads, but only as a flavoring to the dressing or as a rub against a wooden bowl, not, in most cases, as an ingredient.

If a herb has a strong flavor, such as tarragon or basil, you do not need very much of it to give a salad some zest. A teaspoon to a tablespoon of the herb will do. Simply mix the herb in with the other greens.

Provençal Salad

This salad is something like a Niçoise, which is not surprising since Nice is close to Provençe, or perhaps part of it (depending on your definition of Provençe). The main difference is in the exclusion of such ingredients as potatoes and green beans and the inclusion of rather more herbs. Like a Nicoise, this salad makes a good lunch by itself.

Total Time: 15 minutes
Serves eight as starter,
four to six for lunch

1 1 can anchovy fillets, chopped
3 7-ounce cans of water-packed tuna

2 ¾ cup chopped celery
1 small onion, chopped
½ green pepper, chopped
1 clove of garlic, smashed and chopped
½ cup parsley, chopped
2 sprigs thyme, leaves only
1 fresh bay leaf, chopped finely
1 teaspoon chopped rosemary
¼ cup chopped black olives

3 ½ cup olive oil
2 tablespoons wine vinegar
Several grinds of black pepper

4 Tomato wedges
Whole black olives
Quartered hard-cooked eggs

1. Put the anchovies and tuna (**group 1**) in a salad bowl. Separate the tuna into bite-size chunks if necessary.

2. Add the **group 2** ingredients to the **bowl**, and mix thoroughly.

3. Mix the oil and the vinegar (**group 3**). Toss the salad again, adding pepper (**group 3**) to taste.

4. Garnish the bowl or individual salad plates with tomato wedges, black olives, and quartered eggs (**group 4**).

Cole Slaw

I was turned off cole slaw by the little paper cups that come with so many items in inexpensive restaurants. My wife taught me that cole slaw does not have to be like that. I now count cole slaw among my favorite salads, although I still refuse to eat cole slaw that comes in little paper cups. Here is a version that is definitely *not* to be served in little paper cups.

Total Time: 1 hour
Serves six to eight

1 3 cups shredded cabbage
½ cup chopped green pepper
2 teaspoons caraway seeds
1 teaspoon chopped parsley
1 tablespoon chopped onion
1 clove of garlic, crushed and chopped
1 teaspoon chopped tarragon leaves

2 ¼ cup olive oil
2 tablespoons wine vinegar
Several grinds of black pepper
½ teaspoon dry mustard

    1. Combine the **group 1** ingredients in a large bowl.
    2. Combine the **group 2** ingredients in a measuring cup, and mix well with the cabbage combination. Chill for at least half an hour before serving.

Index

Index